GAME and FISH

From Field To Table

Also by the author:

Fish and Game Cookery
The Contemplative Angler
This Was My Valley

GAME
and FISH
From Field to Table
by Roy Wall

The Naylor Company
Book Publishers of the Southwest
San Antonio, Texas

Library of Congress Cataloging in Publication Data

Wall, Roy.
    Game & fish from field to table.

    1. Cookery (Game)   2. Cookery (Fish)   I. Title.
TX751.W34   641.6'9'1   76-183417
ISBN 0-8111-0442-7

To all of those who go afield
and care about their kill or
catch, I dedicate this book.

Foreword

If there ever was a need for someone to come forward with a plea for care of game in the field, this is the time — when modern life is hectic for the occasional hunter, and the non-hunter who tastes his field fare complains the meat wasn't worth the effort.

It's been a difficult job for those of us who know better to convince the anti-hunting public of the heritage involved, that hunting is a highly beneficial game management tool, and that the taste of the game can be worth the discomforts and expense the true outdoorsman will experience happily for his sport.

So it's with appreciation that I listen to Roy Wall's comments about keeping game meat palatable. After all, the experienced butcher and restaurant chef makes your beefsteak dinner worth the money. The hunter shouldn't expect to treat his game with inexperienced callousness and have the meat compare with the butcher's product.

I have known Roy Wall for many years. If I should choose someone to promote conservation and cookery in the same breath from among the outdoorsmen of this nation, I undoubtedly would think of Roy Wall. I recommend a close reading of this book's sage advice to all outdoorsmen worth their shell casings, and then I wish you happy taste buds at your next meal of venison, duck or pheasant.

W. S. (Bill) Billieu

Outdoor Editor, *Wichita Eagle and Beacon*
Board Chairman, Outdoor Writers of Kansas
Vice-President, Great Rivers Outdoor Writers
Member, Outdoor Writers Association of America
Board member, Citizens for Environmental Action in
    Kansas, etc.

Contents

Introduction

For years, I have been deeply concerned over the lack of care given game and fish in the field. And, I regret to say, my concern has increased perhaps one hundred fold over the past ten years. Why? Because I have seen literally tons of game go through regular check stations that was spoiled beyond salvaging. The American pioneer, living on the fringe of civilization where game and fish were immeasurably more abundant than they are today, would abhor this neglectful and wasteful practice. Certainly, there was waste among the pioneers for man is a very wasteful predator, and millions of buffalo were slaughtered just for their hides. But because of necessity, the pioneer learned to preserve food and later there were smokehouses and meat poles which became essential adjuncts for every settler's clearing. Our forefathers depended upon game and fish for food — food that was harvested from the land on which they lived. Obviously, this frugal way of life was all that the pioneer required or we would not be around today.

But why have we neglected to follow the teachings of our forefathers? Has our civilization, waxing fat on the abundant natural resources of this great land gone so completely modern that the housewife gathers food in a shopping basket at the supermarket and nowhere else? Have we been conditioned to equate food with money and the killing of wild creatures as a fringe benefit that is justified because we have paid for a license? Regardless of how tall our skyscrapers are, how often we go to the moon, man is irrevocably linked with the soil and if he loses sight of this fact he violates the law of survival.

Man's instinct to hunt and fish is a way of life and has been through the ages. This instinct has survival value — it is basic in the will to live. But why has man lost the desire to care for his kill? He still likes to hunt and fish but he fails to follow through after his kill is made. Is man conditioned to modern food processing? Is man's instinct to kill more dominant than his desire for food?

There is something else that has bothered me. For years, I have deplored the complete lack of understanding of the way to prepare game and fish for the table. Why is it that the housewife is convinced that there is some sort of mystery, a kind of hokus-pocus about the cooking of wild meat and even of fish?

During the hunting season when my telephone rings, more often than not it is a housewife who wants to know my secret for preparing game for the table. The conversation usually goes something like this: "My husband likes to hunt and he drags in stuff and expects me to cook it so it is fit to eat. I soak it in vinegar, in brine, in milk, but the results are awful. What else can I do? Can you give me your secret?" "Have you tried Lysol?" I ask. No word from her since.

I do not give any of these housewives secrets on cooking game for I have none. But, when it is possible, I give their hunters a lecture on the proper care of their kill before the good wife has to prepare it for the table. But even when wild meat is properly cared for before and during cooking there are those who declare that it is something less than delicious. Is it conceivable that modern man's palate has become so totally conditioned to the flavor of domestic meats where controlled diets determine their flavor that the flesh of wild game which has fed on uncontrolled diets is foreign and distasteful? When such is the case the cook can and often does bury the "wild" flavor with such pungent spices as bay leaf, sage, garlic, etc. It seems to me that this is the wrong approach. Why not educate the palate or stop killing the game?

Hunters may highten their pleasures afield in the study of the habitat where they hunt their game. For example, many hunters who go after deer in the western states hunt the foothills because the going is easier. The deer in this area browse primarily on sage, cedar, and rabbit brush which do not contribute to the flavor of the meat. A bit of scouting would reveal that scrub oak and acorns, quaking aspen, willows and other browse grow just a little higher in the hills, and they all make for delicious venison.

This is just one example, but almost every species of game, mammal or bird may present an interesting study, the outcome of which might well improve one's attitude toward the goodness of wild game.

In summation, I am not suggesting that we return to the smokehouse and the meat pole era; nor am I suggesting that the housewife become a gourmet cook. I merely ask that the man who hunts and the woman who cooks be fair to whatever he kills and she prepares. In other words, I sincerly hope that the reader will find in the pages that follow the key to broader fields of recreational pleasure.

Roy Wall

Part I

The Basic Principles of Cookery

Somewhere far back down the trail over which man has struggled to become civilized he discovered, quite likely by chance, that the flesh of his kill was more palatable when it was subjected to the action of heat. Just when primitive man made this most important discovery is too remote to speculate upon, but we may be certain that the art of cookery evolved ploddingly and tenaciously from this ancient beginning and, like the other arts, the art of cookery has progressed from a crude beginning to its modern elaborate process.

Today, racial food patterns are well established the world over, in fact, nations have survived by them; and the boundaries of palates are as sharply drawn as are those of religions and customs. I shudder when I imagine a smorgasbord for Americans that might include bird nest soup from China; raw fish and sliced cucumbers from Japan; frog legs, garnished with the purée of snails, from France; fricassee of iguana, garnished with the eggs of the big lizard, from Guinea; snake meat salad, with a dressing of

1

termites and honey, from aboriginal Australia; roast turtle, with a sauce of decayed fish, from the South Sea Islands; and many other dishes that are relished by mankind in various parts of the world. But it isn't necessary to understand the palates of the world in order to appreciate wholesome delicious foods. And, in learning to prepare such foods, it is necessary only to observe a few cardinal principles in cookery and to be diligent and patient until a moderate amount of skill is acquired; the results will be gratifying.

Let us examine the most important fundamentals of good cookery. To begin with, all foods have a characteristic flavor that we either like or dislike, and these flavors should be preserved and protected during the cooking process. In short, the best method for cooking any food is that method which imprisons and retains the original flavor. All too often the flavor is cooked out of the food instead of into it. When the juices of meat, for example, are imprisoned within and the meat is allowed to cook in its own juice, it isn't necessary for one to be an epicure to realize that the meat has retained its individual flavor. This is good cookery in any land, or so it seems to me.

A rather prevalent impression exists that just any sort of food eaten out of doors is appetizing, but such an idea should be examined. I, for one, have seen served and often have been obliged to eat camp or picnic food that would tax the digestive equipment of a goat. Moreover, rarely if ever have I heard anything but high praise for such culinary muddling.

To begin with, monotony is inimical to the nature of man and not only the sort of food but the manner and environment in which it is served can become so tedious that it cloys the appetite. Furthermore, man is a dynamic energetic creature built for exercise; exercise burns up energy, and food furnishes the fuel for energy. Man is supposed to work for his food and in doing so he takes the best tonic for his appetite. But civilization has so altered our way of life that we rarely exercise sufficiently to develop

2

fully our normal inheritance of good sound bodies, to say nothing of keeping them in tune as vital going concerns after maturity.

Is it any wonder, then, that a day spent in the woods with its varied routine, invigorating surroundings, fresh air and exercise should engender a voracious appetite? There are many things which contribute to the joys of eating and not the least of these is the companionship and conviviality associated with good food. Certainly, there are few occasions where fellowship finds greater zeal than in the camps of hunters or fishermen.

Since man's beginning, he has either hunted for food or for a job that would furnish him with the wherewithal to procure his food; and so today, when he goes into the wilderness with rod or gun, the age-old instinct of survival takes possession of him and he counts as a prize that which he is able to catch or shoot. Well do I know that prideful feeling which comes over me when my camp larder is bountifully supplied with fish and game. And my pride doesn't stop with a full larder for my prizes must be properly cared for and prepared for the table in the most delicious way.

Needless to say young meat is tender and old meat is tough and, in some species of game birds and animals, the old meat is strong or acrid in flavor. The sportsman who bags a noble head, a monarch of a wilderness glade, has a just right to be proud but in so doing he imposes double duty on the camp cook for, in most cases, the finer the head, the tougher the meat. However, if the animal is in good condition, the loins of an older critter will be tender enough to broil, the hams can be roasted, and the balance of the carcass can be braised and stewed.

With the exception of soups and stews, where the juices must be extracted, the first cooking operation is to be sure the albumin has been coagulated. This may be accomplished by searing over extremely ardent hardwood coals, cooking in boiling fat, in tumbling water, or on a very hot iron griddle or frypan.

To a great extent the meat and its degree of tenderness must determine the proper method for cooking. For most meats that are tender, and some species of fowl and fish, broiling and roasting are superior methods of cooking because these methods preserve the natural flavor of the food. The tougher cuts of meat and the older fowl and small game should either be braised, baked, boiled, steamed, or made into stews.

Meats that are to be cooked for stews and soups should be put in cold water and allowed to come to the simmering point and held there until all of the juices have been extracted. If it isn't allowed to boil dry, it is difficult to cook a stew too slowly or too long. But avoid cooking the meat to "a rag." A hurried stew is a very flat insipid affair. The moral is: Never cook a stew when you are in a hurry.

I have long since avowed that the product of the frypan has contributed more to America's indigestion, unless it is the sandwich, than any other comestible that comes from the American cuisine. However, when the frypan is used properly, and I might add, wisely, it has its place in cookery. In fact, the camper would find it most difficult to get along without it.

Certain species of fish, young fowl and small game may be cooked by frying or sautéing. Frying in deep and very hot fat sears the the outer surface of meats and thus prevents them from becoming grease sodden; it also preserves the natural juices. Small or thin fillets may be sautéed in a little fat, but the heat must be greatly reduced and held constant.

Remember to always have meats dry on the outside before cooking as the juices will escape from wet or water-soaked flesh. Never test or turn meats by piercing with a fork during the cooking process for this will break the seal. Don't add cold water to boiling meats as this reduces

4

the heat and arrests the cooking process. If water is to be added be sure it is boiling.

Stuffing birds with cold dressing or plastering them with a coating of dough is an unwise practice as the juices and thus the flavor of the meat escape into the dressing or dough which leaves the bird dry, flat, and tasteless. Moistening the dressing with some of the stock after the bird has been cooking for a time and baking it separately is a good method to use.

Never salt meat before cooking for it will draw out the juices rapidly. Salt broiled and roasted meats after they have been cooked. When frying in deep fat, salt and pepper may be added to the flour, corn meal, or bread crumbs in which the meat was rolled before cooking. When baking, boiling, or braising, salt a few moments before serving, allowing the meat to continue cooking just long enough for the salt to penetrate the food.

When roasting large fowl or large cuts of meat over an open fire, it is best to build an auxiliary fire to one side so that ardent coals and not additional wood may be added to the roasting fire. Adding wood where roasting or broiling is being done arrests the process of cooking and the flame smokes the meat.

Basting, especially roasting meats, is always a good practice as it keeps the outer surface moist; use either the drippings or a sauce with an oil base. Fish, fowl, and meat, like the haunch of venison, and small game should be well greased with lard or oil before broiling, roasting or baking. This coating aids in searing the outer surface.

Of course camp cookery isn't as foolproof as is that of the modern kitchen (where you may prefer to do your cooking) and it is contingent upon a knowledge of good cookery and the proper management of fires. This knowledge may be acquired by observation and diligence, if there is the desire.

One of the first lessons the inexperienced camp cook has to learn is the management of the fire. It is difficult for

5

him to realize, until sad experiences have taught him better, that a small bank of hardwood coals produces enough heat to cook a sizable meal and that a bed of hot ashes will keep a kettle of beans or stew simmering all afternoon. All too often the novice camp chef attempts to broil over a bed of softwood coals and before the meat has started to broil the heat has diminished until only a few fluffy, cold ashes are left for a vagrant breeze to catch up and scatter over pots and pans and food. Then there is the blazing inferno which makes charcoal of all of the food and sears the cook for good measure. These, of course, are the two extremes. In between is the ideal cooking fire, and a little patience will soon teach the observing person how to build and manage the amount of fire that is needed to prepare food in a wholesome efficient manner. Much of the food prepared over a campfire might be considered rather crude and even unpalatable, if it was served anywhere else. This isn't because the campfire is crude or inadequate; the fault is with the cook. In fact, to me no modern cooking device can equal the campfire when it is properly managed.

Part II

Big Game

Venison is a term generally applied to the flesh of all species of the deer family which includes deer, elk, moose, and caribou. For the sake of convenience and because the flesh of the game isn't so dissimilar as to require a different way of cooking, it might be well to also list here the pronghorn antelope and the wild sheep.

The pronghorn antelope, one of America's most unique animals, was on the verge of extinction at the turn of the century but rigid protection and habitat improvement came to its aid and it is now found in considerable numbers in several of the western states and Canada.

The wild sheep are species of American big game which are very near extinction and it is possible that these noble dwellers of the high peaks will soon disappear from the sportsman's schedule.

Fortunately, the bear, that is both the black and the cinnamon (which is a color phase) are on the increase in much of their native habitat. But the grizzly and its relatives,

7

the Alaskan Brown and the Kodiak, have been reduced to the special province of the trophy hunter.

Care of Big Game in the Field

When the hunter makes a kill the first thing to do, before the pictures are taken, is to bleed and draw the animal. If the head is to be saved for mounting the animal should be bled by sticking it at a point just to the left and slightly back of the apex of the brisket. Slashing the throat injures the scalp and while the slit can be repaired the head is definitely marred.

To draw, roll the animal over on its back and put logs or rocks on either side to hold it in this position. Slip the point of the hunting knife under the skin directly in the center of the top of the brisket and slit the skin for several inches in a lengthwise cut. Don't cut through the abdominal wall; turn the knife, cutting edge up, and rip the skin straight down the center to the vent. With the fingers, aided occasionally by the knife, roll the skin back for three or four inches on each side of this incision. Now, with the skin rolled back out of the way so the objectionable loose hair can't get on the meat, slip the knife, cutting edge up, through the abdominal wall just forward of the pelvic bone (being careful not to puncture the intestines), and cut an incision large enough to insert the free hand into the cavity. With the free hand in the cavity keeping the intestines out of the path of the knife, rip the abdominal wall straight up the center to the lower point of the brisket bone. If the animal isn't too old, the pelvic bone can be severed without a great deal of difficulty. There is a cartilaginous seam or joint directly in the center of the pelvic bone and if the blade of a heavy knife can find this seam the joint can be severed. Make the cut from the front of the pelvic bone, put all of the weight of the body on the knife and rock back and forth. When the bone is severed, open the carcass by breaking the hind legs down.

If the brisket bone can't be split, cut the diaphragm or dividing membrane between the chest and abdominal cavity free from the ribs on either side and after severing the windpipe and gullet clean the entire visceral cavity by pulling and cutting the contents loose from the carcass. Save the heart and liver; remove the gall bladder from the liver, if the animal isn't a deer. The deer is unique in that it doesn't have a gall bladder.

To avoid bone souring, elk, moose, caribou and bear should be skinned out as soon after drawing as possible; if the carcass is too heavy to hang, the meat should be quartered and gotten off the ground and put on logs or bushes so the air can circulate to all areas. Ofttimes, in the case of these larger animals, only the saddle and hams are taken; the balance is left for the wolves and coyotes or, perhaps, it is used as bear bait. This is not only a wasteful practice, but it is an ignominious and illegal practice.

Before skinning, if the animal is a deer, remove the musk glands on the inside of the hock joint, being careful to cut wide of the gland to avoid the musk, and wipe the knife well before continuing the skinning operation. Now, split the skin on the inside of the legs in a straight line from the belly incision to the hock or tarsus joint of the hind legs and to the knee or carpus joint of the front legs; peel the skin off the carcass with the knife and the knuckles of the fist; grasp the loosened skin from underneath on the hair side with the free hand just at the point where it still clings to the carcass and with the knife or the fist pull out and down on the freed skin, keeping the skin taut and the field of operation clear to work. When possible use the knuckles of the fist in a rolling downward and outward motion. This method of skinning is particularly successful on the flat surfaces such as the sides, back, hams and shoulders; and it avoids cutting the skin which often happens when a knife is used. Sever the knee and hock joints; leave the skin intact below the joint if the feet are to be used to make a gunrack, a hatrack, or for any other

9

purpose. To avoid getting the carcass dirty, keep it on the skin as you work.

Since deer and antelope are much smaller than elk, moose, caribou, or bear, the body heat escapes more rapidly, which lessens the chance of bone souring and for this reason these animals (after bleeding and drawing) may be taken into camp before they are skinned. If they are hung in the shade where the air can circulate and the rib cage is spread open with a gambrel stick crosswise inside the carcass, there should be no problem in keeping the meat for some time.

Most hunters who are successful in hunting bear are more interested in a bear rug than they are in a bear roast and for this reason care should be taken when skinning the animal. Slip the knife under the skin (cutting edge up) at the base of the lower jaw and split the skin straight down the belly to the vent, being careful not to cut through into the abdominal cavity. From this cut, slit the skin on the inside of the legs to the center of the pads of all four feet and finish skinning the carcass the same as you would that of a deer. Skin the feet out carefully, being sure to keep the claws intact. The head, however, must be skinned so as to preserve the nose pad, ears, eyelids, and lips. Measure the skull from the nose to its base and across its greatest width. The taxidermist usually prefers to use a plastic skull but if you want to preserve the original, remove the tongue, trim off all of the flesh that you can, chisel a small opening at the back, being careful not to fracture the skull, and remove the brains. Now, boil the skull slowly in a kettle of water until all of the meat and cartilage can be rubbed off. Avoid overcooking for it will weaken the skull at the seams. Remove all meat and fat from the skin and salt well, especially the scalp, the nose pad, the lips, and the base of the ears and feet. Fold, flesh sides together, roll and put in a cool drafty place.

Removing the Cape for Mounting

Special care should be taken in removing the cape if

the head is to be saved for mounting. A deep shoulder mount is much more desirable and, to be sure there is enough skin for such a mount, sever the cape from the balance of the skin by cutting from a point several inches back from the point of the shoulder straight over the withers to the same position on the opposite side, cutting from the flesh side to avoid disturbing the hair. When the cape has been removed, make a cut up the back of the neck to a point directly between and in line with the base of the ears and cut at an angle from the end of this center incision to the base of each antler, forming a V at the back of the head. Sever the cartilage of the ears at the neck, then cut the scalp free from the bony base of the antlers and skin down to the posterior edge of the eye sockets. It is at this point and also when removing the skin from around the muzzle that great care should be taken so as not to cut the skin. Care should also be taken not to injure the eyelids. For example, just below the deer's eye is a deep pit or the lachrymal gland; to avoid cutting the scalp here, work slowly, always being sure that the knife travels close to the bone. At the nose, cut deep into the cartilage; be careful to cut close to the bone when skinning around the lips. After taking the measurement of the skull from its base to the tip of the nose, the antlers may be removed by sawing horizontally from the occipital bone at the back of the head straight through to the nasal bone in front and taking the dome of the skull off with the antlers. Cut away all clinging flesh and fat from the cape, spread out and salt well, putting considerable salt around the eyes, nose, lips, and the base of the ears; fold flesh sides together and roll; keep in a cool dry place.

After removing the cape, split the neck from the point of the brisket to the base of the lower jaw and remove the windpipe and the gullet. This is important, especially if the whole carcass is to be saved, for meat spoils rapidly around this area. When a buck deer is in the rut, his neck

11

is enlarged and the flesh is unpalatable. If your kill is such an animal, sever the neck at the shoulders and discard.

The Aging of Game

The flesh of either wild game or domesticated animals and fowl can be improved by aging, but there should be a limit to the aging process. A case in point is the bear. Bear meat isn't unlike pork in that it is very fat and rich, and extended periods of aging will cause it to spoil, and refreezing for long periods will cause it to become rancid. As for venison, it should be hung for several days before it is processed for the freezer.

If the weather is fairly cool and the altitude is above 5,000 feet, it is an easy matter to keep meat in good condition by hanging it in the shade and where the air can get to it. Sometimes the blowflies will be active during the warm part of the day, but these pests work close to the ground and if the meat is hung twenty feet from the ground there is little danger in its being molested. Watch closely to see that no soft wet spots or blood clots appear and if they do dust them with finely ground black pepper.

Of course this business of hanging game for a long time depends upon the weather, locality, and altitude. Fall hunting camps from 5,000 to 8,000 feet rarely experience difficulty in keeping game hung for a limited period of time. Lower altitudes, where there is increased humidity, increase the chance of spoiling and game must be used as soon as it has cooled out or put in cold storage.

Among the peoples of the world there is a great variety of tastes— tastes that can't always be accounted for. At one time in the history of mankind, a particular food and the way in which it was prepared might have been nutritionally important; or, maybe a ritualistic ceremony dictated the diet. But there are other tastes which stem either from remote times or are so hopelessly lost in the centuries of the struggle for existence that no basis for any of them is possible to establish. And so, whenever and wherever the question of the aging of game is discussed there will be varying opinions. For example, some prefer to cook their game while it is strictly fresh; others contend that it is ready for the pot just as soon as it is thoroughly cooled out; and there are those who insist that all game should be frozen for a week or longer before it is ready to cook. Game that has hung until it is ripe or high, until the weight of the bird pulls the head off or the tail feathers out, is too high for my palate, I must admit. But aging in the open air for ten days or more is most beneficial to domestic and wild meat alike.

There are two agencies that cause decay or spoilage of unprocessed foods: (1) microorganisms, which come from contamination, and (2) enzymes, which already exist in the living tissue. Microorganisms can be greatly reduced by careful handling, by cleanliness, and by avoiding the use of water. Enzymes can't be avoided, however, for they are a part of the living tissue and remain after death. In short, microorganisms or bacteria are living forms of plant life which attack nonliving food from the outside; whereas enzymes are chemicals that are already present in food and attack it from within. The chemical function of enzymes in dead tissue is a process that is known as autolysis, or self-digestion. It is this leavening or self-digesting process which breaks down the tissues and improves the meat when it is carefully and properly aged. To be sure, the aging process shouldn't be carried too far for the meat will spoil. Don't forget that weather conditions and altitudes greatly influence the outcome of aging game, for low temperatures retard the action of both microorganisms and enzymes, and high altitudes reduce humidity and lessen the danger of mold and other bacteria.

It is quite important that meat that is to be aged should be cooled out as rapidly as possible; if this isn't done, the slow withdrawal of the animal heat may produce bone souring, which is a bacterial infection down next to the

13

bone. For this reason, game should be dressed and hung in cool or cold air just as soon as possible.

Ventilation is a most important factor in aging meat, especially if the temperature is high or, say, above freezing. But here again altitude makes a difference. For instance, in freezing weather at low altitude when the air is heavy and damp, decomposition will progress more rapidly than it will at a temperature of fifty degrees Fahrenheit at an altitude of 5,000 or 6,000 feet. The meat may be encased in a cheesecloth sack which will prevent dehydration to some extent. Examine it carefully every day or two for soft spots that may show up, especially in the areas where the tissues have been broken by shot or bullet. When such spots appear, they should be trimmed off or out and the place rubbed well with a mixture of corn meal, salt and black pepper.

During extremely cold weather when game is likely to freeze solid, it is well to wrap the meat in paper and store it in the tent, cabin, car, or house, provided the place isn't too warm. Once meat has been frozen, decomposition, after thawing, progresses more rapidly.

Ofttimes the hunter, because of necessity or otherwise, is in a hurry to eat a portion of his kill. When this happens, the desire for food takes precedence, and not how long the game should be hung. However, no meat should be cooked until it has thoroughly cooled out — until all of the animal heat has been withdrawn.

Finely ground black pepper is an excellent repellent for flies and a good supply of this pungent spice should go into camp. The pepper should be dusted on the surface of the meat, especially in moist places. Flyblows won't hatch on the dry surface, but the moist spots must be watched if the weather is warm enough for flies to be about. It is here that the black pepper is most effective and it should be used freely, particularly in and about crannies and folds. Encasing the meat in cheesecloth helps to keep it clean and also protects it from flies.

14

When in camp it is often desirable to preserve a portion of meat for some time. This isn't a difficult job if the following mixture is used: Take 3 pounds salt, 4 tablespoons allspice, 6 tablespoons finely ground black pepper, 1 cup brown sugar. Mix thoroughly and keep in a friction top tin can or pail. Cut the meat into chunks no larger than five or six pounds; rub a liberal portion of the above mixture on each piece and work or massage it into the meat with the hands. Hang the meat out of the sun and where the breeze can get to it. Repeat this operation daily for three or four days, then hang the meat in a cool dry place. It will keep well and taste even better a month after preserving.

When big game has been properly cared for in the field and in camp, the next step is the locker plant. Usually there is a locker plant in the hunting area where you can take your kill and have it processed before you transport it to the locker in your home town. At this point, may I suggest the following:

Trim all of the tallow from the meat because this is where the objectionable taste comes from when the animal hasn't fed on a controlled diet. Moreover, fat freezes at a much lower temperature than meat and it becomes rancid and causes the meat to be unsavory.

When a deer or antelope carcass has been sawed down the backbone, divide and package it for freezing in the hams, the shoulders, the two loin strips, and the ribs. The processors at the locker will wrap the meat in freezer paper which prevents freezer burn. All too often the hunter tells the locker butcher to cut the loin into chops and make "deerburger" out of the balance of the carcass — tallow and all. This is venison at its worst. The chops are usually wafer thin, they dehydrate badly when frozen, and the "deerburger," with its fat, will become rancid and altogether unpalatable. If the meat has been frozen in the larger pieces, as suggested, it will retain its original goodness. As a

15

general rule, elk doesn't carry much fat so the trimmings can be ground for "elkburger."

Before cooking the loin, first thaw, then bone by removing the "eye" of the loin from the backbone. This strip can be broiled over the coals, entire, or sliced into fillet mignon one inch thick and wrapped in a strip of bacon, then broiled.

With a meat saw sever the ribs three inches from the backbone, then saw into five-inch strips crosswise the ribs. These rib strips are delicious when broiled over slow heat and basted occasionally with your favorite barbeque sauce.

The above suggestions apply to the deer and the antelope; since the elk is a much larger animal its carcass must be cut into smaller pieces to accommodate the freezer locker. Bone the hams and cut into portions that are convenient for wrapping; cut the loin into four pieces and the shoulders into portions that are suitable for roasting. The ribs can be sawed crosswise and stacked for wrapping.

If the above suggestions have been followed, steaks that are cut an inch thick from the hams, fillet mignon from the loin, the ribs, and the burgers can be broiled over the coals in the brazier on the patio or in the backyard and served with a vegetable and a salad which complement the meat; and your family and friends will understand why you go hunting.

Part III

Big Game Cookery

To start with, let me repeat that there is no mystery associated with the cooking of any game, even though there is an all too prevalent idea to the contrary. I've wondered if this attitude stems from the fact that we are conditioned to going to the market where we see meat nicely packaged, after it has gone from the slaughterhouse to the Saran Wrap. Furthermore, we fail to realize that all meat has to go through a process of preparation before it is ready for the cook.

When meat is slaughtered and cared for professionally, it reaches the cook with all of its goodness. When game is bagged, it is cared for by the careless, the ignorant, the neglectful; but fortunately, it is also cared for by the concerned and the knowledgeable sportsman. It is difficult for me to admit, but the sportsman who cares is outnumbered by those who are indifferent, and it is because of this fact that the care of game has been given special and detailed consideration in this book.

After you have read what I wanted to say on this matter I hope you will agree with me that there is no mystery associated with game cookery; that if you can broil a beefsteak to your satisfaction, you can broil a steak from big game. There are absolutely no secrets connected with this operation; all one needs to do is to follow the rules for good cookery. And this same principle holds true for any game dish. Therefore, in offering the recipes which follow I do so with the full knowledge that today the ready mix products are available to either the camp or the housewife shopper.

May I also add that the word venison is used here to include other members of the deer family, i.e. elk, moose, and caribou; and also, the antelope. And so the recipes that follow can be adapted equally well to the meat of all of these animals.

Broiled Fillet Mignon of Venison

Bone out the loin strip from a relatively young animal that has been well aged. Peel off the tough membrane that is on top of the strip and cut the required number of fillets 1 inch thick. If the animal is small, the fillets can be cut butterfly — that is, they can be cut 2 inches thick and slashed in the middle which doesn't sever them but allows for a 1-inch thick double or butterfly fillet. Rub with bruised garlic; brush with oil and broil on a brazier over hot coals or over campfire coals for 10 or 12 minutes to the side. Avoid overcooking.

Serve with sliced, tart, unpeeled apples that have been sautéed in butter and sprinkled with sugar and a dash of cloves, allspice, and cinnamon. A tossed green salad goes well with this food.

Broiled Venison Ribs

Cut 4-inch strips of ribs crosswise with the camp ax or saw; wipe clean with a damp cloth and brush with oil

18

or melted lard. Broil slowly on an open grill over medium-hot coals, turning several times. The low heat will help to render the fat which sometimes gives a rank taste to the ribs. If the heat is even, broiling time should be about 10 or 12 minutes to the side. Make a swab for basting by wrapping a clean white strip of cloth on the end of a peeled sweetwood branch and baste the ribs often with your favorite barbeque sauce, or, if you wish to make a different sauce, see the recipe below.

Serve the ribs with sauerkraut, corn bread and black coffee.

Barbecue Sauce

Into a pint Mason jar mix ½ teaspoon freshly ground black pepper, 1 teaspoon dry mustard, 2 cloves garlic that have been bruised to a paste, 1 teaspoon salt, a dash of thyme and tabasco. Add ½ cup vinegar and ¾ cup salad oil. Set aside for an hour, cap and shake well before using.

Venison Stew in Wine With Cottage Cheese Dumplings

Bone out the shank end of the ham or heel of the round and trim well, being careful to remove the tough sinews that are associated with the hamstring. Dice 2 pounds of the meat in 1-inch cubes.

Pour 2 cups red wine (not port, which is too heavy) into an enamelware or earthenware utensil; add 1 medium-sized sliced onion, 2 chopped blades celery, cut strips of 1 green pepper, 2 finely minced cloves garlic, thin slices of 1 carrot, 2 sprigs parsley, a bunch of celery tops, ½ teaspoon freshly crushed black pepper, 1 teaspoon salt, and 1 bay leaf. Now add the venison; be sure that it is all emersed in the marinade; cover and put in the refrigerator or on the back porch, if the weather is cool enough. Let the meat marinate for several hours or, better still, overnight. To make sure that all of the meat is marinating, stir often with a wooden spoon. (Any metal container or spoon affects the flavor of the wine.)

To cook: Lift the meat from the marinade and drain well in a colander. Put 4 tablespoons oil in a stew kettle; place over low fire; roll the venison cubes in flour and brown lightly in the hot oil; mix in the marinated vegetables, but don't brown them. Add 2 cups of the marinade to the meat and vegetables; cover and reduce heat so the stew simmers, and only simmers, for 1 hour. When the liquid has reduced, add the rest of the marinade and continue to simmer until the meat is tender. If there is too much liquid, remove the lid and increase the heat to a boil, stirring often to avoid sticking.

Serve on the same plate with stew, cottage cheese dumplings over which some of the wine sauce has been poured.

Cottage Cheese Dumplings

Put one 12-ounce carton of small curd cottage cheese into a mixing bowl; add 2 eggs and stir until well blended; sift in enough flour to make a dough stiff enough so that it has to be pushed with the finger from the spoon. Have a stewpan ready with slowly boiling salted water and another containing cold water. Drop a rounding teaspoon of the stiff dough into the gently boiling water. When the dumplings come to the surface, lift them out with a strainer spoon and lay in the cold water for 10 or 15 minutes. Thirty minutes before serving, lift them out of the cold water and place in a Pyrex dish with melted butter. Heat in a 250⁰ oven for 20 minutes.

Kabobs of Venison

Bone out the rib eye and strip off the tough membrane that covers its top side. Now cut pieces 2 inches long; their thickness will depend upon the thickness of the strip of the rib eye.

Cut a long, slender, green stick, being careful to select a sweet wood such as willow, sassafras, hickory, or aspen; peel off the bark and sharpen the small end. These wooden skewers are actually the best, unless you have a silver-plated metal skewer; the ordinary metal type often gives food a metallic taste.

Have at hand several slices of bacon or a chunk of salt pork; cut the bacon in 3-inch strips, or the salt pork in ¼-inch thick, 2-inch pieces. Impale the salt pork or bacon (which should be folded once in the middle) on the skewer; follow with a cube of venison. Continue alternating the bacon and venison until half the skewer is filled; brush with oil and sear over hot coals, reduce the heat and continue to broil for 10 or 12 minutes, turning several times to expose all of the kabobs to the heat. Broiling time depends upon the thickness of the kabobs; take care, however, not to overcook. Season with a touch of salt, unless pork is used, and black pepper.

Serve piping hot with mint sauce or currant jelly, drop biscuits, and baked potatoes.

Drop Biscuits

Take 2 cups sifted flour and sift again with 4 teaspoons baking powder, 1 or 2 teaspoons sugar, 1 teaspoon salt. Using the fingers, gently mix in 5 tablespoons oil; add enough milk to make a dough that is stiff enough to spoon out onto a greased baking sheet. Bake in 400⁰ oven for 12 or 15 minutes.

If in camp, use Dutch or reflector-type oven; preheat Dutch oven over coals; baking time should be about 15 minutes. To brown top of biscuits, fire the lid with live coals.

Preparing Baked Potatoes in Camp

Forty-five minutes or an hour (depending upon the size of the potatoes) before the meat is ready to serve, clear the hot ashes and coals from a place in the fire bed; dig a small pit about 3 or 4 inches deep and large enough to accommodate the potatoes; put them in the pit and cover with hot ashes and rake the fire over them. Build up the fire, if need be. About 35 or 40 minutes later, test the potatoes with a sliver of sweetwood. When they are done, rake them out of the ashes and keep them warm near the fire until ready to serve.

Roast Shoulder of Venison

If you aren't equipped to do the following, ask your butcher to do it for you; it will take him only a few minutes.

Select the shoulder of a relatively young animal or an older one that has been well aged. Square the shoulder by severing the neck, then saw back of the shoulder at the back line down through the brisket and through the ribs to a point several inches below the point of the shoulder. Trim and wipe clean with a damp cloth; rub well on both sides with oil; put in a roasting pan and place in a 350⁰ oven. Add no water and don't cover. Roast for 1 hour then baste with barbecue sauce. If you prefer to make a sauce, see recipe for broiled venison ribs. Roasting time will vary, but 3 hours should do the trick. Twenty minutes before taking from the oven, season the roast with salt and freshly crushed black pepper.

Serve with scalloped potatoes and onions, mint sauce or a tart jelly, and a tossed green salad topped with slices of fresh tomatoes.

Scalloped Potatoes and Onions

Peel and thinly slice twice as many potatoes as onions. In a buttered baking dish, put first a layer of potatoes then a layer of onions and salt and pepper; repeat until all of the vegetables have been used; add 1 cup milk, dot top with butter and put in the oven for 1 hour before roast is done.

Venison Curry

Put 3 tablespoons melted butter, lard, or oil in a heavy skillet that has a close fitting lid. When butter is hot, add 2 cloves finely minced garlic and 2 medium-sized sliced onions; cook until slightly browned. Stir in 1 heaping tablespoon curry powder; when thoroughly mixed, add 1 cup canned tomatoes and ½ cup raisins; let simmer for 10 minutes; if it cooks down too much, add a little boiling water. Set aside where it will stay warm.

Take about 1 pound of meat from a venison shoulder and cut into inch cubes. Grease another skillet; put on fire; when hot, drop in the venison cubes and sear until brown. Add the cubes to the onions, tomatoes, etc.; season with salt, cover with boiling water or stock and allow to simmer slowly until meat is very tender, or about 1½ hours. When the liquor cooks down, add just enough stock or water to keep the meat covered.

Serve with plain boiled rice.

Venison Chili

Trim 2 pounds of lean venison from the shoulder or tag ends of the rib eye and cut into small pieces no larger than 1-inch cubes, Heat 4 tablespoons oil in a heavy kettle; when hot, put in the meat and brown slightly. Reduce the heat and add 1 medium-sized, finely chopped onion, 4 or 5 cloves minced garlic (depending on the size), 2 cups tomato juice or canned tomatoes, 3 rounding tablespoons chili powder, ½ teaspoon ground cumin, a dash of oregano, and a can of consommé. Reduce heat and simmer, and only simmer, for an hour, or until the meat is tender. Add boiling water if the liquid is reduced too much.

23

If you are at an altitude of 4,000 feet or below and you like beans (frijoles) with your chili con carne, put 1 cup dry pinto beans to soak the night before you prepare the chili. Next morning, start the beans in cold water and bring to a boil, then reduce heat and let them simmer for several hours, or until soft; add to the pot of chili. The time for cooking the beans depends on the altitude, for beans don't respond to boiling at high altitudes.

Serve with tortillas (the commercial ones are acceptable) and a green salad.

Venison Stew

There is one dish that is always welcome in camp or at home and that is stew. East and west, north and south, the name may change but, as Webster puts it, it's usually "a dish of meat and vegetables." Perhaps in no other phase of cookery does the camp "chef" have a greater opportunity to let himself go than when he prepares his mulligan, ragout, burgoo, skilligalee, slumgullion or just plain stew. And, even though the "chef" is allowed culinary latitude in the extreme, and though difficult to believe, I have never known of a fatality as a result of partaking of one of these ambrosian monstrosities. Digestive tablets and sleepless nights, yes, but no deaths.

As we have said, there are many variations in preparing this staple camp or home dish, and it isn't our desire to inhibit any ambitious chef; hence, we go down the middle of the road with the following recipe:

Cut 2 pounds of venison from the shoulder, brisket, flank, lower ham, of any tag ends of good solid meat. Cut into 1-inch cubes, rub with salt and crushed black pepper; add ¼ pound diced bacon, salt pork, or ham; place all in a kettle and cover with cold water. Bring to a boiling point then reduce heat and allow to simmer for 1 hour, or until meat is almost tender.

The vegetables and spices that are added will depend

upon what is at hand, but potatoes and onions are staples, and they are basic elements of any well-planned stew. Peel and quarter 4 medium-sized potatoes and 3 onions. Dice coarsely 4 carrots, 4 sticks celery, and 1 green pepper; add 2 cloves minced garlic, a dash of thyme, 5 peppercorns, 1 tablespoon vinegar or lemon juice, a scant teaspoon each of sugar and salt.

When the meat is almost tender, add the spices and all of the vegetables except the potatoes; let simmer; 40 minutes before dishing up, add 1 medium-size can tomatoes and the potatoes and continue to cook until the potatoes are done.

Roast Ham of Venison

Select the ham of a relatively young deer or antelope that has been aged. Saw the shank bone several inches above the hock joint and trim carefully, being certain to trim off all of the fat and fibrous tissue. Wipe clean with a damp cloth and brush both sides and the ends with oil; place in a large roasting pan; add no water and don't cover. Put roast in a 350⁰ oven and roast for 1 hour, then baste well with your favorite barbecue sauce or, if you wish to prepare one yourself, see the recipe for broiled venison ribs. A small deer or antelope ham will weigh 8 or 10 pounds, and roasting time will be about 15 minutes per pound. Puncture the ham to the bone on the thick side with a sliver of sweetwood or a piece of wire; if the juice shows pink the meat is done. Don't overcook.

Serve with sliced mushrooms sautéed in butter, stuffed baked potatoes, mint sauce, and a tossed green salad.

Stuffed Baked Potatoes

Select the required number of medium-sized shapely Idaho potatoes, scrub clean with a vegetable brush, rub lightly with lard, and put to bake for about 40 minutes in a moderate oven. When cool enough to handle, halve lengthwise and remove the pulp with a spoon, being careful not

25

to break the skin. Put the pulp in a mixing bowl and add salt and pepper to taste, a lump of butter, a generous amount of grated Cheddar cheese, and enough milk to enable you to whip the potatoes. Now fill the half-shells with the whipped potatoes; round up the tops and sprinkle with finely chopped parsley. Put to bake in a moderate oven for 30 minutes.

Broiled Venison Liver

Wash, trim, and skin the liver of deer or elk; slice the required amount in 1-inch slices and brush with oil, if broiling over coals; if oven broiling, preheat a shallow pan in which there are several tablespoons of oil; dip first one side of the liver and then the other into the hot oil and broil for 20 minutes in a 450⁰ oven. If broiling over coals cook for 12 minutes on one side and 8 minutes on the other. To test, stick the point of a knife into the liver; if the juice is pink, continue broiling until the juice shows clear. Season with freshly crushed black pepper and salt.

Serve with buttered onions, baked potatoes and a green salad.

Buttered Onions

Peel and chop the required amount of onions (usually 1 of medium size is served to the individual). Put a frypan over a slow fire, add 3 tablespoons melted butter; add the onions and season with a pinch salt and a little sugar; cover with a close fitting lid. The onions should not stick or brown, so check them often. Add 1 tablespoon boiling water occasionally to keep the butter from burning. The onions are done when they are tender and clear. Be sure to let all water cook off, leaving only the buttered onions.

Venison Mincemeat

It has been my experience that venison makes superior mincemeat, and I offer here the recipe which I use.

From the shoulder and tag ends of the brisket cut 2 pounds of good solid meat; put through the food grinder, using the coarse blade. Add ½ pound finely chopped beef suet, 5 pounds chopped tart apples (winesaps), 3 pounds raisins, 1 pound currants, 1 cup chopped, candied orange peel, and the same of lemon peel, 2 cups chopped citron, 4 cups brown sugar, 2 teaspoons each cinnamon, allspice, cloves, mace, 1 teaspoon salt and 1 of black pepper, 1 cup each of apple juice, orange juice, pineapple juice, grapefruit juice, ½ cup lemon juice, 1 ½ cups water. Cook slowly for 2 hours, stirring often. Seal in jars.

Before baking the pie, sprinkle 2 tablespoons brandy over the mincemeat before the top crust is added.

Bear

All bears have omnivorous diets and they eat a great variety of food. Ground squirrels, grubs, nuts, roots, herbage, wild fruits, fish, cattle, sheep and, unfortunately, carrion and garbage dumps are all welcome food to the bear. Whether domestic or wild, the flesh of all edible creatures is affected primarily by the food they eat. Because of the varying conditions of both seasons and districts, animals with omnivorous diets are often forced to live on foods which don't contribute to the goodness of their own flesh. This is definitely true of the bears. There is a vast difference between the flesh of a bear that has been feeding on acorns and wild fruits and one that has made too many visits to the putrefied carcass of an elk, moose, horse, or other animal. However, if a young bear, say one that is two or three years old, has been living right, its meat isn't bad fare, especially if it is marinated before it is cooked.

Marinade for Bear

Into an enamelware or earthenware utensil put the juice of 2 or 3 lemons or limes, the juice of 1 orange, 1 cup vinegar, 3 cups red wine (not port) — cider may be used, 1 sliced onion, 1 diced carrot, 2 sticks diced celery or a handful of celery leaves, 1 finely minced clove garlic, 4 sprigs parsley, 1 bay leaf, 2 seeded and veined chili peppers and a generous dash of nutmeg. Lay the meat in this marinade and let it stand in a cool place for 8 or 10 hours, turning and basting frequently.

Broiled Bear Chops

Remove the chops from the marinade and wipe dry; broil over the coals and baste frequently with some of the marinade. Cooking time will depend upon the thickness of the chops, but be sure they are well-done.

Serve sautéed apples with this dish. Corn bread muffins should also be included for they are a staple with this food.

To prepare the apples: Leave the peelings on the fruit, core and slice medium thick. While the apples sauté in a little butter, sprinkle them with sugar and any spices that are desired.

Roast Bear

The shoulders, loin and hams may be roasted in the oven the same as pork is roasted. Remove from the marinade and wipe dry before putting in the oven. Like pork, these cuts of bear should be well-done.

Serve with corn bread muffins, baked yams, mustard greens and a tossed green salad.

Part IV

Small Game

The hunter's small game bag includes the cottontail rabbit, the snowshoe hare, the jackrabbit/hare, the fox and gray squirrels and, occasionally, the more unorthodox raccoon, opossum, muskrat, marmot and beaver.

Rabbits and Hares

The several species of cottontail rabbits might be considered the number one game animals in the nation. However, hunting them as a sport is rather tame. Rabbits are prime when winter has possessed the fields for a few weeks, for it is then that they are fat and tender and the flesh is almost pearl white and delicious. In late summer and early autumn young rabbits that are fried like young chickens are very good. This is especially true of the several species of cottontails that are found in the mountains, in the plains and in the mesas of the West.

Although the hunter looks favorably upon the rabbits

29

as food, the hares (with the exception of the snowshoe) aren't too well thought of; and the jack hares or jackrabbits (as they are generally but erroneously called) are rarely sought. Young hares, however, are tender and their flavor is quite agreeable when they are properly prepared. When an older jackrabbit/hare is taken during the winter months and aged, the saddles aren't without merit, especially if they have first been marinated.

Care in the Field

Rabbits and hares should be bled and drawn just as soon after killing as possible. Don't use the knife when skinning but grasp the skin below the hock joint and pull downward. The skin will peel off easily. Keep the hair rolled back from the exposed flesh to avoid getting hair on the meat. Hang to draw; split the brisket up to the point of the sternum then split the pelvis and clean out from the top downward; wipe clean with a dry cloth, paper, or grass.

Squirrel

Although there are many species of squirrel that are distributed over most of the temperate and tropical regions of the world, it is chiefly in America that they are hunted for sport and for food. Squirrel hunting may not be high adventure, but there are many gunners who enjoy the sport. The flesh of the squirrel is considered delicious by many; to others it is gamy. Of course, much of the flavor depends upon what the animal has been eating.

Our founding fathers initiated squirrel hunting, and the long barrel muzzle-loading squirrel rifle is a part of early American history. The squirrel pie once served at the Cold Spring Club, the City Tavern, and other early-day ordinaries that were situated in and about Philadelphia, attracted many of the great men who fashioned eighteenth century American history. These ordinaries were famous for their food and squirrel pie was often on the menu. Here, such dignitaries as General Washington, Alexander Hamilton, Patrick Henry, Robert Morris, and others frequently dined while they discussed the affairs of state.

The species of squirrel that are usually hunted are the fox and the gray; the Abert, which is found in the high country of the West, is occasionally sought by the hunter; the small red squirrel or chickaree and related species, are too small and gamy to be of much value as food.

Care in the Field

Anyone who isn't familiar with the job of skinning a squirrel can easily make work out of this simple operation. Just grasp the animal by the tail and, with the thumb and the blade of a knife, pluck the hair from a spot just under the base of the tail. Cut through the skin and sever the tail bone and then cut on each side at an angle toward the flank. One well-directed slash on either side will accomplish this trick, but be careful to see that the slashes slant toward the flanks. Now lay the squirrel on the ground, belly up, put your foot on the tail well up toward the body, grasp the hind legs and pull upward. The skin should peel off toward the head, tearing to a V-shape on the belly. Catch the tip of this V-shaped skin and pull upward, peeling the skin off the hind legs. Slip the skin off the shoulders, forelegs and head as you would strip a shirt off over your head. Draw as you would a rabbit. A little practice will soon develop skill and this skinning operation can be done quickly and neatly with no hair getting on the flesh. The phase of this job that requires the greatest attention is the first two cuts, one on each side of the base of the tail, for, if the skin isn't slashed at an angle toward the flanks, the tail is certain to tear off, leaving nothing to hold to. If this happens, cut the skin on the back of the animal and slip the fingers of both hands into this slit and pull in opposite directions, peeling the skin off from the center toward both ends.

Raccoon

Heading the list of the more unorthodox game species is the raccoon. In some localities in the deep southland the raccoon or coon, as it is referred to by its admirers, vies with the possum in popularity. And they are very easy to take care of. All one needs to do is to skin, draw and carefully clean; remove the kernels in the small of the back and under the front legs; cool out by hanging for several nights in the open air.

Opossum

The opossum is the lone representative of the order of marsupials or pouched animals in America; the balance of the clan is confined to the Australian region. If we are to learn of the delectableness of the opossum we must go into the deep, deep southland where possum an' 'taters is a proverbial *piece de résistance* of the southern Negro.

Blessed or cursed (according to the point of view) the opossum has a very flexible appetite. His menu includes mice, rabbits, birds, insects, eggs, poultry, fruit, green corn (of which he is particularly fond), nuts and carrion. When autumn comes with its frosts and flaming fields, the wild persimmon is ripe and succulent and it is then that the opossum prepares himself beautifully for the roasting pan.

Because of this wandering appetite of the opossum, whenever it was possible, I have taken the animals alive and penned them up for ten days or longer and fed them milk and bread and table scraps. Such a diet not only sweetens the meat but it helps to make certain that it is in as prime condition as possible.

In preparing the opossum, first bleed it by sticking with a knife just at the point of the brisket. Don't skin, but scald and scrape as you would a pig; have water in a large kettle or small tub just slightly below the boiling point. Grasp the opossum by the tail and immerse him in the hot water, turning him over and over, allowing the water to

32

scald the entire surface. Pluck at the hair every few seconds and when it slips readily on all parts of the body lift the body out of the hot water and immerse it for just a moment in cool water and, with the edge of a knife, scrape off all the hair. Now pour cool water over the carcass repeatedly and continue to scrape until the skin is very clean and white. Remove the head and draw as you would any other animal.

In the small of the back there are two little reddish kernels or glands which should be removed; the same is true of the two glands that are under each foreleg or armpit. Make an incision under each foreleg; you will find the gland lying between the shoulder and the ribs.

Hang the opossum out of doors in a drafty, cool place; if there is a heavy frost at night, you may be certain that your kill is getting the best of treatment. The more frost it gets, the better.

Muskrat

What about the muskrat? Well, I once asked a guide in the north woods, a man who possessed enough worldly goods to live very comfortably, what sort of wild meat he considered to be the most savory. Without a moment's hesitation, he answered, "Young muskrat." If you believe this statement, it might do no harm to experiment on your own. In case you do and you have luck, simply skin the animal, draw, and clean only the hind legs and saddles very carefully. These are the choice parts. Be sure to remove, without breaking, the musk sac and the kernels that are in the small of the back. Hang the meat in the frosty air for two or three nights before cooking.

Marmot

Any of the several species of marmot can be eaten, and they may be prepared in the same manner as muskrat and beaver.

33

Beaver

A young beaver isn't bad fare, and his tail is quite good. Simply draw the animal, skin and carefully pare; be certain to remove the kernels in the small of the back and under each foreleg that are between the ribs and shoulders. Hang in the open air for several frosty nights.

The raccoon, opossum, muskrat, marmot and beaver should be taken during the cold months only. It might also be well to point out that no flesh is edible if the animal has been caught in a steel trap and thus subjected to the stress of anger, fear, and pain, for the endocrine glands become active and the meat's goodness is destroyed.

Part V

Small Game Cookery

The following recipes for preparing small game animals, which include the more popular rabbits, squirrels and hares, as well as the less popular raccoon, opossum, muskrat, marmot, and beaver, may be prepared at home as well as in camp.

Fried Rabbit With Cream Gravy

The rabbits should be killed and dressed at least two days before cooking. Clean and wash thoroughly and cut into neat joints convenient for frying; season with salt and pepper; dip in milk; roll in flour and fry in deep hot fat until rich brown. Put in a casserole without covering and place in a moderate oven for 20 or 30 minutes.

After frying rabbits, drain off the fat and add 1 or 2 tablespoons melted butter and 1 heaping tablespoon flour; cream into a smooth paste then add 2 cups milk, stirring continually to avoid sticking. Season with salt and pepper and simmer over a very slow fire until gravy thickens.

Drop biscuits (see page 21) should accompany this dish to the table.

Rabbit Pie

Wash, clean and joint two rabbits. Place rabbit pieces in a stewpan with just enough boiling water to cover; cook about 20 minutes and add 1 cup diced cured ham. Reduce heat and let simmer until the meat can be stripped from the bone. Remove from fire and let stand until cool enough to handle; take all of the meat off the bones and return to broth in which it was cooked.

Mince very fine 2 sprigs parsley and 1 small onion; add to the meat. Season with salt and pepper and simmer 15 minutes longer.

Make a pastry as follows: Into 1½ cups flour put 1 teaspoon baking powder, 1 teaspoon salt, and sift at least twice. Take shortening the size of a small egg and work it gently into the flour with the fingertips; slowly add about ½ cup cold milk or water, or enough to make a smooth dough. Turn dough out on well-floured board and roll out thin enough to line a buttered baking dish. When the rabbit meat has cooked down until the broth has thickened, pour it into the baking dish. Beat 2 eggs in 1 cup milk and pour this over the meat. Roll out the balance of the pastry and cover the dish, perforating the top dough to allow the steam to escape. Place in a 400⁰ oven and bake until crust is brown.

Rabbit, Mexican Style

To serve four or five persons take two rabbits that have been carefully cleaned and cut into pieces convenient for frying. See that the meat is thoroughly dry.

Remove the seeds and veins from 2 chilies; if dried ones are used, soak them in cold water until soft. Into a frypan put a generous amount of fat; when hot, drop in the chilies; fry until brown, pressing occasionally to extract the pepper flavor. Remove chilies and discard. Rub each piece of rabbit lightly with a touch of garlic paste and drop into the hot chili fat. When golden brown place the rabbit in a casserole or covered baking dish; set aside in a warm place while the sauce is prepared as follows:

Pour off the fat in which the rabbit was cooked; add 2 tablespoons melted butter; when hot, add 1 finely diced carrot, 1 finely chopped small onion, 3 tablespoons chopped green pepper, 1 cup chopped mushrooms. Cook over a slow fire until almost done, being careful not to brown; add 1 heaping tablespoon flour and cream well with vegetables. Now to this add the following: 2 cups poultry or beef stock (water can be used), the juice of 1 small orange, 1 heaping tablespoon peanut butter, ½ teaspoon ground cumin, 1 tablespoon sesame seeds (that have been toasted by shaking in a dry frypan over a slow fire), 3 cloves, 3 slices orange peel, dash of nutmeg, and salt and pepper to taste. Let simmer until thoroughly blended (about 10 minutes); salt the rabbit and pour over it the blended sauce from the frypan. Put 3 or 4 sprigs of parsley on top of the meat and bake in moderate oven for 1 hour, or until meat is tender.

Potatoes baked in their jackets are excellent with this dish.

Rabbit Curry

Prepare the rabbit as in the recipe for frying. Dip each piece in milk, roll lightly in flour, and brown in hot fat.

In another frypan, lightly brown 1 diced onion in a little hot butter; add 1 heaping tablespoon curry powder, blend well; add 1½ cups beef or poultry stock, milk from 1 large coconut, ¼ cup lentils (previously soaked in cold water for 8 or 10 hours), and a small bay leaf. Let this sauce simmer for 30 minutes over a slow fire; add the pieces of browned rabbit, cover with a close fitting lid, and simmer for 1 hour, or until the meat is solid but very tender. Keep the fire low and stir occasionally to prevent sticking. Twenty minutes before serving season with salt.

Serve with boiled natural brown rice.

Broiled Young Rabbit

Clean carefully two young rabbits; leave them whole but flatten by breaking the ribs and legs outward to facilitate the broiling process. Brush with oil and put to broil over a bed of ardent hardwood coals, using either the open wire grill or folding type. Baste frequently with the following mixture: 1 teaspoon freshly crushed black pepper, ½ teaspoon salt, 3 tablespoons vinegar, 2 tablespoons oil. Broiling time is about 20 or 25 minutes, but the size of the rabbits and the constancy of the heat make the broiling time vary. Be certain, however, that the meat is well-done.

Potatoes boiled in their jackets, peeled and browned in butter, may go to the table with the broiled rabbit.

Hares

Young hares may be prepared the same as the rabbit. The following recipes, however, are offered in addition.

Kabobs of Hare and Bacon

Bone the loin of a young hare, either snowshoe, jack hare, or other species. The fillets are easily removed by running the point of a sharp knife along the sides of the backbone from the top downward, cutting down to the transverse process of the vertebra, then cutting outward to free the long round fillet from the backbone.

Cut fillets into pieces about 1 inch long. For each piece of hare, cut a piece of salt pork, or bacon 1 inch square by ¼ inch thick. Now cut about 3 green, sweetwood branches 2½ feet long; peel and sharpen at both ends. On the smaller end, skewer first a piece of hare then one of bacon, another piece of hare, and so on until you have skewered 4 pieces each of hare and bacon, starting with hare and ending with bacon. Skewer the balance of the meat on the other branches. Sear well over very hot coals, then stick the larger end of the branches in the ground in front of a reflector fire, leaning them toward the fire so as to get the benefit of the constant heat. Turn the branches occasionally to expose the meat equally to the heat. Roast about 10 or 15 minutes, taking care not to have the heat too great which will burn the bacon. When well-done (and they should be well done), remove from the skewers onto a preheated pan, salt slightly, allowing for the salt on the bacon or salt pork, and add a liberal dash of freshly crushed black pepper.

Hare With Chili

Bone out not only the loin as suggested in the preceding recipe but the rest of the hare as well. Cut the meat into cubes. Into a hot kettle or deep frypan drop 4 or 5 pieces bacon or salt pork; when it sizzles, add the cubes of hare, and sear. As soon as the meat is well seared, pour enough hot water over it to cover, put on a tight fitting lid and simmer over slow fire for 30 minutes, then add the following: 1 slightly rounded tablespoon chili powder, 2 cloves finely minced garlic, and ½ teaspoon ground cumin. If dried whole chilies are to be used, they should be soaked in cold water until soft and the seeds and veins removed before they are added to the meat. Let the meat simmer for at least 30 minutes or even for an hour.

If frijoles are to be served with the chili, put 1 cup of dry pinto beans to soak in cold water the night before the chili is prepared. Next morning put the beans over a slow fire. One hour before they are done, add 1 chopped onion, 2 cloves minced garlic, 1 cup tomato juice or canned tomatoes, 1 tablespoon chili powder. Let simmer until well blended, then add chili.

39

Marinated Hare

The flesh of the hares, especially the wild species, is usually stronger in flavor than that of the rabbits. For this reason it is ofttimes advantageous to marinate the meat before cooking. Prepare the marinade as follows:

Take 1 cup white or red wine (cider can be used), 2 tablespoons vinegar, 1 stick coarsely chopped celery, 1 diced carrot, 1 sliced onion, 3 sprigs parsley, 1 bay leaf, 1 clove minced garlic, 5 peppercorns, juice of 1 lime and 1 orange, pinch or two of nutmeg, a few slices of orange peel and the same of green pepper.

Divide the hare into neat joints, clean well, wipe dry and arrange in a flat earthenware dish. Pour over it the marinade and let stand overnight, turning the meat when possible to expose all of it to the marinade.

Just before removing the hare from the marinade, dice 1 small slice of ham, or several slices of bacon and brown lightly; when almost brown, add 1 sliced onion and let cook for about 5 minutes, without browning.

Season the marinated hare with salt, roll in flour and brown the pieces in another frypan. Now add the hare to the marinade that has been strained, cover with close fitting lid, simmer slowly for 1½ or 2 hours, or until meat is tender. Stir occasionally to prevent sticking; if liquid cooks down too much, add a little hot water from time to time.

To serve, arrange the pieces of hare in the center of a hot platter and pour over them the liquid in the pan. Garnish with mushrooms that were cooked in butter. Macaroni is also an excellent dish to serve with hare.

Boiled Macaroni

Boil the macaroni in tumbling salted water until it is almost tender. Drain well and put in buttered casserole; pour at least 1 cup milk over it; finish cooking in a moderate oven.

Squirrel

Before cooking squirrel, be sure to remove the kernels or glands in the small of the back and those under each foreleg between the ribs and the shoulder.

Squirrel Stew With Dumplings

Squirrel, not unlike other meats, may be prepared in many ways, but certainly, stewing with dumplings (noodles or macaroni can also be used) is one of the best. In fact, when the squirrels are prime, squirrel stew is equal, or even superior, to any stew I have ever eaten.

After removing the kernels, joint each squirrel into 6 pieces, that is, the forelegs, hind legs and back, which is halved. Put the pieces in a stewpan, season with salt and pepper, cover with cold water, place over slow fire and simmer until meat is very tender but solid — that is, not cooked to a rag. Remove the meat from the broth and set aside in a warm place.

There should be at least 4 cups of broth left; add hot water, if needed, then add the dumplings, noodles, or macaroni. When they are done, add the squirrel and simmer a few minutes before serving. The noodles and macaroni, of course, can be bought but the dumplings will have to be made.

Drop Dumplings

Into 1 cup flour put 1 scant teaspoon baking powder and the same of salt; sift twice. If drop dumplings are desired, add enough milk or water to make a stiff dough that has to be pushed from the spoon with the fingers. Push from the spoon into the simmering broth, cover with a tight fitting lid and let simmer for 20 minutes without removing the lid.

41

Fried Young Squirrel

Select only young squirrels for frying. Clean and joint them as in the preceding recipe. Into a heavy iron skillet put plenty of frying fat and heat until it is almost smoking hot. Dip each piece of squirrel in milk, season with salt and pepper, roll in flour, and drop into the hot fat. Fry to a rich brown and drain on paper. Keep piping hot.

If gravy is desired with the fried squirrel, pour off the frying fat from the skillet, add 2 tablespoons melted butter, 1 heaping tablespoon flour, and cream to a smooth paste, allowing the flour to brown slightly. Now add 2 cups milk, or water, and simmer for 5 minutes, stirring all the while to prevent sticking. Season with salt and pepper and serve in a gravy bowl with the squirrel.

This is a wonderful breakfast dish, especially on a cool morning. Biscuits and a tart jelly should also be included.

Braised Squirrel

Select reasonably young squirrels; clean well and flatten by breaking the ribs and legs open, but leave whole. Brush with oil or lard; place in a folding broiler or on an open wire grill; sear over a bed of coals in the brazier, then broil. Baste frequently with a mixture of crushed black pepper, salt, a few tablespoons oil and a tablespoon vinegar. When the squirrels have broiled to a nice brown, put them in a roasting pan, add just enough hot water to keep them from sticking, cover and bake in a moderate oven until the meat is tender. Add additional hot water, if needed.

Raccoon and Opossum

The raccoon and opossum are two species of game animals which find great favor with the people of the South, and because the method of preparation for the table is interchangeable, the recipe given below works equally well for both animals. As we have suggested in the preparation of game, if the meat has hung for several nights in the frosty air before cooking, it is greatly improved. I might add also that the opossum is much richer and not unlike young pig and the excessive fat can become objectionable unless it is skimmed off in the process of roasting.

Roasted Raccoon or Opossum

Into boiling salted water, put 1 sprig sage or bay leaf, 1 onion, 2 pods seeded and veined chili peppers; add the animal and boil for a little less than 1 hour.

Select 3 or 4 good-sized Puerto Rican yams and boil in their jackets. When almost tender, peel and cut in half the long way.

Now take the animal from the boiling water, drain well, lay in a roasting pan and put in a 300° oven for ½ hour, then surround the meat with the yams and sprinkle them with ginger, cinnamon, cloves and brown sugar or cane syrup; return to the oven and roast for another ½ hour.

Serve with this dish turnips and their tender greens that have been cooked with a liberal slice of salt pork or pig jowl and, of course, corn bread or pone.

Muskrat and Marmot

Both of these animals can be prepared in much the same way. As we have said before, hanging them for several nights in the frosty air before cooking improves their flavor.

Ragout of Muskrat or Marmot

Put 1 sliced onion, 1 pod seeded and veined chili pepper, 1 bay leaf and any variety of herbs you care to add, into a kettle of boiling salted water. Drop in the animal and allow to simmer slowly until almost tender. Lift from the water, drain and wipe dry before putting in the baker. Lay 2 or 3 slices of salt pork or bacon across the meat and add enough boiling water to prevent it from sticking. Cover with a tight lid and cook slowly until tender.

Broiled Muskrat or Marmot

Before broiling, the animal should be parboiled as in the above recipe. Brush over with oil or lard and broil on a brazier or campfire coals for 15 or 20 minutes or longer. Serve with this dish your favorite vegetables.

Beaver

Although an old beaver has an unpleasant flavor that is rather similar to the bark of an ancient water-soaked log, young beaver should not be overlooked entirely, especially if the meat has hung several nights in the frosty air.

Roasted Beaver

Parboil the meat in tumbling salted water for 1 hour, brush with oil and roast either on the brazier or over the coals of the campfire.

Serve with any vegetables that are at hand.

Beaver Tail

Take the tail and impale it on a sharpened stick and roast for several minutes over the coals. When the rough skin begins to blister, take the tail from the fire and, when cool enough to manage, peel the skin off. There will now be a piece of gelatinous meat which should be roasted over the coals, or boiled in tumbling salted water until tender. To me, the flavor of beaver tail is quite acceptable.

Serve baked potatoes with this meat.

Part VI

Upland Game Birds

The upland game birds of this country offer the hunter the greatest of sport and a day afield is a day to remember, whether one hunts quail, grouse, turkey, doves, wild pigeons, or the three introduced species which include the pheasant, the chukar partridge and the gray partridge. Every species of upland game has its champion and I must admit that the bobwhite quail has my vote, not only in the field but as a delicacy as well.

Quail

The bobwhite, the scaled, the California or valley, the Gambel's, the mountain and the harlequin or Mearns' are the several species of quail in this country and all of them are great game birds. Furthermore, because of their white meat which has a most delicious and delicate flavor when it is prime, they are held in high esteem by all those who have eaten them.

Perhaps the bobwhite is the best known and the most popular of the entire group, and it has a number of outstanding qualities which justify its distinctive position. It has wide distribution in accessible cover; it lies well for the dog; it freezes tight; and it presents a worthy target for the gunner. The combination of these facts gives the hunter an opportunity to spend a delightful day afield with beautiful dog work and companionship that remain in one's memory long after the hunting season has passed.

Grouse

There are numerous species of grouse that are found in America but unfortunately destruction of habitat and excessive hunting have so greatly reduced every species on this continent that their future is doubtful and, in some cases, extinction is certain unless there is rigid protection and environmental improvement.

A few of the dominant species that this group of noble upland game birds includes are the ruffed grouse, the dusky grouse, the spruce or Canada grouse, the sharp-tailed grouse, the pinnated grouse or prairie chickens, the sage grouse or sage hen; and the rock, the white-tailed, and the willow ptarmigans.

With the exception of the sage grouse, the flesh of these birds is highly prized. The sage grouse feeds so extensively upon wild sage that its flesh is most unpalatable, especially that of the old birds. Young birds that are taken in late August or early September aren't so affected if they are drawn immediately. In fact, they are quite good.

Pheasant

The propagation of the pheasant, especially the ring-necked species, dates back to the Roman Empire. This unique distinction, to my knowledge, belongs only to the pheasant. The pheasant's popularity spread to England and centuries later to America. Richard Brache, an Englishman who married the only daughter of Benjamin Franklin, brought the first pheasants from England and planted them on his estate in New Jersey. This initial attempt to acclimatize so exotic a game bird to American game coverts failed, but subsequent experiments proved successful and today the ring-necked is well established in such states as the Dakotas, Nebraska, Minnesota, Iowa, Wisconsin, Ohio, Pennsylvania. In fact, it is doing well in much of that portion of the continent which lies between the fortieth and fiftieth parallels that are below 6,000 feet.

With the rapid decline in the population of our native grouse the successful introduction of the pheasant has been a boon to the American gunner, even though it isn't comparable to our native grouse as a game bird or as a table delicacy; nor does the flesh have the wild flavor that is characteristic of the grouse, instead, it is rather tame. In truth, the pheasant is little more than a glorified barnyard fowl, what with its centuries of association with man. And its greatest contribution to the gunner is the fact that it responds well to the controlled shooting areas where hatchery birds may be released.

Turkey

On an afternoon in early November not so long ago, I sat leaning against the trunk of a great spreading live oak. The oak and cedar clad hills of southwest Texas fanned out against an autumn sky in a sea of green and gold and yellow with tiny islands of coral dotted here and there where the frosts had splashed the sumac to a flaming red. Before me lay a small parklike clearing at the far end of which stood a spring pool that was fringed with yellow willows where wild turkey came for water just as twilight laid a dusky finger on the quiet valley.

I had been waiting under the live oak for perhaps an hour and all had been quiet save for the distant lowing of cattle down the canyon, the raucous cry of blue jays in the dark cedars and the soft prattle of white-crowned sparrows in the bush nearby. And then, at the far side of the clearing, noiselessly, like a bronze shadow, a magnificent gobbler stepped out of the bordering thicket. With all of his baronial bearing, he surveyed the surroundings. As I found him over the sights of my rifle, a vagrant breeze toyed with the old fellow's long black beard. The crack of the rifle split the silence that was hovering over the little glade, the bird spun in his tracks and disappeared. Hurriedly I crossed the opening to where I had last seen him and there he was, the grandest of American game birds. Something clutched at the inside of me when I picked him up and most of the thrill was gone.

Later, when friends gathered with me around Thanksgiving's festive board, the fine old gobbler, as rich brown as the autumn oak leaves he knew and loved, graced the centerpiece. I picked up the carving knife and started to serve when something tugged at my emotions. I caught the tang of autumn scented woods at twilight, saw again a bronze shadow float out into a little clearing, the gallant head lifted, the body poised and ready for action like sleeping wind in a storm cloud, and I understood why the wild turkey is a bird to remember; I understood why it demanded the respect of the first Americans; why the Pueblos included it in their ceremonial rites; why the Mayas of Yucatan, who domesticated it centuries before the arrival of Columbus, included it in much of their ritualistic life.

When our forefathers came to America they found the wild turkey abundant in areas over nearly half of the United States, and the first Thanksgiving birds were taken by the colonists who used their dependable shooting irons, the flintlock muzzle-loaders. Indeed, colonial America found the great flocks of wild turkey an indispensable source of food on many occasions. But, following in the footsteps of our progenitors and aided by modern firearms, American gunners rapidly depleted this once bountiful stock until today only a few districts may boast of the presence of the wild turkey; and their future now depends upon what use man chooses to make of the few areas remaining where this, the only species of the pheasant family that is native to America, has retreated to wage its last ditch fight against a crowding inimical civilization.

Doves and Wild Pigeons

Because of its wide distribution over the continent and its migratory habits, the mourning dove has gained in popularity with the sportsman in recent years. There is, however, considerable objection to killing them. This opposition stems from a certain sentiment which undoubtedly has its root deep in early ecclesiastical references.

Much less abundant and inhabiting more restricted ranges are the white-winged dove of Texas and Arizona and the band-tailed pigeon of the Pacific states and the Rocky Mountain regions. While these species are larger than the mourning dove, their flesh is much the same and they may be prepared for the table in the same manner.

Chukar Partridge

The chukar partridge (which is native to the Tibetan Himalayas) has been introduced in several of the states but the stocking of this splendid game bird has met with success only in the western states where there is suitable habitat, i.e. an altitude that is above 5,000 feet and arid rocky terrain such as is found in Colorado, Utah, Nevada, California, New Mexico, etc. The chukar has responded well enough in these areas to warrant a limited hunting season. While hunting big game on the western slope in Colorado, I have observed large flocks on several occasions, and always they were in arid, rocky canyons where there was little evidence of either cover or food.

The chukar is a beautiful and excellent game bird. It

lies well for a dog and it doesn't fly far on the flush. Otherwise, it performs in much the same manner as the bobwhite quail. But the chukar is considerably larger and it presents an easy target for the gunner.

Gray Partridge

Another introduced species of the partridge clan is the gray partridge which has established itself very well in the areas of southwestern Canada, in northern Montana and Idaho, and along the Canadian border. It is an excellent game bird and its habits are much the same as the chukar, except that it is found in the more open country along field borders and in grassland. Like other gallinaceous game birds, the gray partridge is a first-rate table bird.

Care of Upland Game Birds

Many hunters, too many, seem to be unaware of the importance of the proper care of their kill, either in the field or in transporting it to the refrigerator. This is unfortunate because killing game should be only part of the true sportsman's pleasure. And so, it is hoped that the simple rules that are suggested below will help some hunters to find out for themselves the added pleasure they can experience on their trips afield if their game is given the care that it is worthy of.

Never skin quail, pheasant, grouse, or turkey unless you want to eat inferior game. Simply dry pluck the birds while they are still warm; when they get cool or cold the feathers will set and the skin will tear. However, the dove is easy to pick any time. To draw, split down the back and empty the cavity, then wipe dry with paper, a rag, grass, or green leaves. Remove the crop, gullet and windpipe by slitting the neck skin.

Never stuff birds in a rubber-lined hunting-coat pocket or game pouch, carry them all day, then throw them in the back of the car and leave them there until you get home. Instead, spread your hunting coat out on the car floor and lay the birds on it; crack the car windows open to allow the air to circulate.

When you arrive at your destination, don't wash or freeze the birds; hang them in a drafty place overnight where they will cool out and be ready for the cook the following day. If the weather is cool and dry, the birds may be hung for several days or a week. If they have to be frozen, put them in airtight freezer bags to avoid freezer burn.

If you can't pluck the birds in the field while they are still warm, just draw them as suggested and hang until they are cooled out, then scald and pluck the day before they are cooked, or freeze as suggested. The day before you plan to cook the birds, remove them from the freezer, let them thaw slowly in the refrigerator, and prepare according to your favorite recipes.

Part VII

Upland Game Bird Cookery

Although individual taste varies in regard to the goodness of upland game birds, it must be admitted that they respond equally well to good cookery, if they are given the proper care immediately after they are bagged.

Quail

All of the species of quail may be cooked in the same manner, and the following recipes can be used for any of these birds with success.

Quail in Deep Fat

After preparing the birds as suggested on pages 50 and 51, leave them whole, dip each one in milk, then roll in flour to which salt and pepper have been added. Have plenty of frying fat in a deep iron kettle or frypan and heat to piping hot. Drop no more than two or three birds into it at a time, otherwise the heat is reduced, which causes the birds to become grease sodden. When they have brown-ed, lift them out with a spatula and drain on paper. Be sure not to use a fork because it breaks the crust and liberates the juices. Put the birds in a casserole or roasting pan and place in a 300⁰ oven for 30 minutes. Add no moisture and leave uncovered.

Drain off the fat from the kettle and add 2 tablespoons melted butter and 1 heaping tablespoon flour; cream with the scrapings in the kettle, then add 2 cups milk and the giblets that have been sautéed in butter and finely minced. Stir continually to prevent sticking; let simmer until thick, season with salt and pepper.

Serve with the quail and cream gravy, hot biscuits and honey.

Broiled Quail

Broiling should not be attempted with quail unless there is an open grate or fire; broiling with gas or electricity is not successful.

To broil, leave the birds whole; rub a little salt and a pinch of freshly crushed black pepper inside; brush with oil and put the birds on a wire grate, then put the grate just above a bed of coals and sear as quickly as possible. Turn the birds often to expose their entire surface to the heat. When the meat is well seared, reduce the coals by half and allow the birds to broil slowly until cooked through, or from 15 to 20 minutes. Turn occasionally to insure even broiling and baste with a mixture of equal parts lemon juice and melted butter.

Boil either wild or natural brown rice; when done, drain and heap it in the center of a large warm platter and circle with the broiled quail. Currant, plum or any sharp jelly compliments this dish.

Quail in Wine

Select eight birds; rub with a little salt and freshly

crushed black pepper; brown lightly in butter or oil; remove from frypan and place in a buttered casserole that has been preheated. Put birds in a 350⁰ oven and pour over them 1 wineglass of white wine.

Now dice 1 carrot, 1 small onion, and 2 tablespoons green sweet pepper; add ½ cup chopped mushrooms and 3 small slices blanched orange peel. Put these ingredients into the butter in which the birds were browned; let cook slowly for 5 minutes, then add 2 tablespoons flour. Blend all thoroughly, then slowly stir 2 cups beef or poultry stock into these ingredients, stir continually so the sauce will be smooth. Season with salt and crushed black pepper.

When the quail have cooked for ½ hour, pour the above sauce over them, cover the casserole and cook for about 25 or 30 minutes, or until the birds are tender.

Serve hot rolls and currant jelly with this dish.

Quail on Toast

Split the back open lengthwise, leaving the breast intact, and flatten as for grilling. Dip in milk, roll in flour, and fry to a nice brown in deep hot oil. Drain the birds on paper.

To make the gravy, pour most of the fat off in which the birds were browned, add 2 tablespoons flour, cream into a nice smooth paste, then add 2 cups milk or, better still, 1½ cups milk and ½ cup cream. Salt and pepper to taste.

For each quail there should be one large oyster. To prepare them, first drain on a dry cloth then season with salt and pepper, dip in milk, roll in flour, brush over with beaten egg yolk, roll in bread crumbs, and brown in hot fat.

Have ready as many slices of hot buttered toast as there are quail; place a quail on a slice of toast and top with an oyster. Sprinkle with chopped parsley.

Serve with this dish, the gravy, hot biscuits, currant jelly and a tossed salad.

Grouse and Pheasant

All of the species of grouse have a gamy flavor but the pheasant is more like a barnyard fowl. Even so, these birds respond equally well to the recipes offered here.

Broiled Grouse or Pheasant

Broiling is an excellent way to prepare these birds, especially if you have an open grate or brazier. Select only young birds; halve them by splitting down the back and through the breast lengthwise. Rub over with melted butter or oil, but don't season. Sear quickly then place on an open wire grill and let them cook slowly until done; turn occasionally, without piercing, and baste frequently with the following:

Mix thoroughly 3 or 4 tablespoons melted butter or oil, add 2 tablespoons tarragon vinegar or lemon juice, ½ teaspoon crushed black pepper and the same of salt.

Sauté the livers, gizzards, and hearts in butter, finely mince and add to buttered rice and serve with the birds.

Grouse or Pheasant With Fillets of Fresh Pork and Broccoli

Place the whole birds in a stewpan with just enough boiling water to cover; reduce the heat as soon as the water begins to boil again and let the birds simmer until tender; lift them from the water and keep warm in the oven.

Cut off the tough ends of the broccoli and remove the woody outer covering of the larger stems; rinse in cold salted water, drain; put in the water the birds were cooked in and boil until tender; drain well and add butter before serving.

While the broccoli is cooking, grill 6 or 8 ¼-inch thick fillets from the loin of fresh pork.

To serve, place the broccoli in the center of a hot

platter, garnish with the grilled pork and surround with the birds.

Grouse or Pheasant With Wine

Rub two of three birds with lard, butter or oil and lay them on an open wire grill and put over ardent coals. When seared to a nice rich brown, place in a roasting pan and pour 2 cups boiling water over them; put in a 350⁰ oven and cover.

The birds should simmer slowly for 15 minutes, then add to them 2 or 3 peeled and quartered medium-sized potatoes, 1 quartered onion, 2 slices orange peel, 6 cloves, 6 peppercorns, 3 quartered carrots, and a pinch nutmeg, if desired. Simmer 15 minutes more and add 1 wineglass white wine and cook until vegetables are done.

Cream to a smooth paste 1 heaping tablespoon flour and 2 tablespoons melted butter. Lift the birds and vegetables from the broth and stir the above into it; let simmer until slightly thickened; if the broth has reduced until the gravy is too thick, add boiling water. Sauté the livers, gizzards and hearts in a little butter, mince and add to the gravy.

In serving, garnish the birds with the vegetables; serve the gravy in a bowl.

Londonderry Sauce is excellent with this dish. (See recipe, page 110.)

Grouse or Pheasant With Bananas

Rub two birds with butter and season inside with salt and pepper; place them in a roasting pan, add 1 cup poultry stock, or water, and 1 wineglass white wine; cover and cook until tender in a 350⁰ oven.

Select 6 firm underripe bananas, peel and slice lengthwise. Melt butter in a flat pan, lay banana halves in it and turn them, cut side up, being careful not to break; sprinkle

57

with brown sugar, and dust with cinnamon, cloves and allspice; bake until the fruit begins to look clear.

The Wild Turkey

If we were not dealing here with the wild turkey it would be extremely audacious to offer suggestions on how best to cook this distinguished bird. However, the wild bird lives a different life and may need different treatment in the kitchen. Although the diet of the barnyard fowl is generally fixed, this is not true of the wild bird. For example, turkey taken from New Mexico where they have fed upon piñon nuts and sweet acorns, are prime; turkey taken from the hill country of Texas during a dry season when there is little to eat but cedar berries, will be strong with cedar oil; and turkey taken from the border country of Texas where they feed extensively upon wild and exceedingly pungent pepper, are flavored with this *Capsicum* herb.

Turkey in Sauce
(Mole de Guajolote)

As we have said, the turkey was first domesticated by the Mayas of Yucatan centuries before the arrival of Columbus, and *Mole de Guajolote* is a traditional dish of the Mexican people — it is a truly exquisite dish which was snatched from the ruins of a glorious civilization that flourished in pre-Cortezian times. I experienced it for the first time years ago and whenever I prepare the food, I recall the unforgettable impact it had on my palate. You can't imagine how delicious and unusual this food is. But I hope you will find out for yourself.

Select a young turkey weighing about 8 or 10 pounds when dressed. Joint it as you would a chicken for frying; be sure the meat is thoroughly dry.

Put about 3 or 4 cups oil or frying fat into a very large frypan, or kettle. Have ready 6 pasilla peppers, 6

58

broad peppers and 3 chilies. If the peppers and chilies are dry, drop them into hot water and let them stand until soft, then open and remove seeds and veins. When the frying fat is hot, drop in all the peppers and chilies and allow them to fry for 5 minutes, then drain on paper.

Now dip the pieces of turkey, including the giblets, in milk, roll lightly in flour, and fry to a golden brown in the pepper-flavored hot oil; arrange in a baking pan, or large casserole; cover with either hot poultry or veal stock; hot salted water can be used instead; allow to simmer gently until almost tender. The liquid should be reduced to half.

Put 1 tablespoon sesame seeds, 1/2 cup pine (piñon) nuts, and 1/2 cup blanched almonds in a dry frypan and toast by shaking over slow heat. Toast 2 tortillas (1 slice of whole wheat bread may be substituted). Put the sesame seeds, pine nuts, almonds, tortillas, chilies and peppers through the grinder (fine blade). Put a little oil in the frypan and slowly fry 3 cloves garlic that have been finely minced. The garlic should not brown. Add to it the following: 2 cups canned tomatoes or 3 large, ripe, chopped tomatoes, 1 bay leaf, 3 cloves, 2 rounded tablespoons peanut butter, the juice of 1 orange, 1 teaspoon cinnamon, pinch each of ginger, thyme, and marjoram, and 1/2 cup raisins. Add the ground peppers, nuts, tortillas, etc., and stir continually until thoroughly mixed. If the sauce is too thick, add some of the broth from the turkey, and simmer over a slow fire for 15 minutes.

When the sauce is thoroughly blended, pour it over the turkey, return the bird to the oven and bake at about 300⁰ until the meat is tender. Move the meat in the pan occasionally to prevent sticking. Just before serving, add 1 ounce unsweetened grated chocolate and blend it into the sauce with a wooden spoon.

Oven Roasted Turkey With Dressing

If the bird is dry picked, drawn but not washed, and

allowed to hang for a week without freezing, it will be superior to one that has been freshly killed or frozen.

Have the bird at room temperature. Don't make the error of stuffing it with a mass of cold, sodden bread and sage, which tends to dry the flesh of an otherwise delicious fowl.

In default of an open grate where the turkey can first be seared, we suggest the following: Clean and singe the bird, being careful to remove the oil sac on the tail. Sever the neck close to the body and tie the neck skin securely. If the crop has been removed by making a slit in the skin, sew it up. Rub the inside with salt and crushed black pepper. Place a handful of celery tops and a few sprigs of parsley in the cavity; sew up the opening and truss; rub with oil, put in a dry roaster, breast side up, and sear in an oven of, say, 550° for 10 or 12 minutes; turn and sear the back. Reduce heat to 325°; add 2 cups hot stock or water; leave uncovered and roast until almost tender — about 2 or 2½ hours for a 10- or 12-pound turkey. Baste occasionally with the stock in the roaster. Season with salt and pepper, and finish cooking, or about 30 minutes. Be sure the bird doesn't overcook; if it was well seared to begin with and the heat is held constant, it will cook in its own juice and will not be dry and tasteless.

Corn Meal Dressing

Crumble 4 cups corn bread and 2 cups whole wheat bread; coarsely dice 3 medium onions, 5 sticks celery, 2 green peppers and put them in a stewpan with just enough water to keep them from sticking; cook until tender, then add to the bread and bind with 2 lightly beaten eggs and 1 cup milk. When the turkey has cooked for about 2 hours, dip 2 cups broth out of the roasting pan and add to the dressing; mix thoroughly with a wooden spoon. Season with salt and crushed black pepper. Put in a buttered casserole and then in a moderate oven for 45 minutes.

Turkey Gravy

Season the giblets with salt and pepper and cook until very tender in 4 cups boiling water. When done, set aside to cool, then chop fine, or grind in the food chopper.

Put 4 tablespoons melted butter and 3 heaping tablespoons flour in a large frypan; cream to a smooth paste over a low fire; slowly add the balance of the broth in which the giblets were cooked, then add the giblets, stirring all the while to prevent sticking. Season with salt and pepper and thin with milk if too thick. If desired, pork sausage, oysters, or chestnuts may be added.

Chestnut Dressing or Stuffing for Turkey

To 4 ounces each of minced veal, cured ham and sausage add 1 medium-sized onion, 12 chestnuts (that have been boiled or roasted), 2 sprigs parsley, 6 cooked and stoned prunes, and 3 sticks celery. Put these ingredients through the food chopper; season with salt and pepper, a little grated nutmeg, 1 tablespoon honey, and 2 tablespoons grated Cheddar cheese. Now heat 3 tablespoons melted butter or oil in a frypan and cook the above ingredients in this pan slowly until they are thoroughly blended. Moisten with 1 cup white wine and bind with 2 eggs. Add 1 cup of the broth from the saucepan the giblets were cooked in, put in a casserole or baking dish and bake in a moderate oven for 1 hour or a little less. (See the preceding recipe for preparing giblets for the gravy.)

Broiled Young Turkey

Young turkeys that will dress about 6 or 8 pounds can be broiled, and they are especially delicious when camp broiled over hardwood coals; a wire grill can be used with complete success for this operation.

Halve the bird by cutting through the back lengthwise,

sever the wishbone at its apex and rip the bird in two; brush with oil and sear over hot coals, first on the cut side, turn and reduce the heat by raking some of the coals off, and continue to broil for 30 minutes or more, depending on the size of the bird. Turn occasionally, without piercing with a fork, and baste often with a mixture of 4 tablespoons vinegar, 2 tablespoons oil, 1 teaspoon freshly crushed black pepper and ½ teaspoon salt.

Chukar Partridge, Gray Partridge, Doves and Wild Pigeons

Because these birds can be prepared in the same way quail are prepared, it seemed best to group them together, looking at it from the culinary side, only. Because the partridges are larger birds, the time allowed for cooking them will naturally be longer, otherwise, the recipes for quail can be used equally well for them.

The flesh of the doves and wild pigeons is dark, of excellent flavor and not overly dry when properly prepared. Be sure to save the hearts, livers, and gizzards, for they contribute considerably when they are first sautéed in a little butter, minced and added to the gravy.

May I suggest frying in deep fat and broiling as especially satisfactory ways to prepare these birds.

Part VIII

Waterfowl and Shore Birds

This wildlife group constitutes a vast array of bird life. While it is possible to eat any of the many species, some of them are much better than others; some are too small to be of any food value; and still others are so unsavory as to be nauseating.

As for the ducks, they can be divided into three groups, i.e. shallow-water ducks, which feed on the surface of the water and in grain fields; deep-water ducks, or sea and bay ducks, which feed on aquatic vegetation, crustacea, etc.; and fish-eating ducks, or mergansers.

The choicest ducks included in the shallow-water species are the mallards, the black duck, the teals (the blue-winged, the green-winged and the cinnamon, which is quite rare), the pintail, baldpate and gadwall. If we suggest that the respective goodness of these ducks is in the order they are given, we not only invite disagreement but we also state only a half-truth, for the flavor of any duck depends upon such factors as locality, time of year, and food.

But it is the canvasback that holds undisputed supremacy in the ranks of the deepwater ducks, especially if it has fattened on its favorite food, wild celery. Following the canvasback is the redhead, the scaups, and the ring-necked.

The last group, the mergansers, are fish eaters and are, therefore, not too palatable. It is possible to eat them, but I assure you the experience won't be remembered with delight.

The same can be said of the coot, the gallinule, and the shoveller, even though they are sought by the gunner, especially along the Atlantic coast.

Of the several species of geese that are found on the North American continent, certainly the Canada goose and its relatives are the best known and the finest of all. The blue goose, the white-fronted goose, the snow goose and the brants (which are now quite rare) follow. These birds mate for life and some of them live to be seventy years old.

The shore birds are many but some of them are on the brink of that dark valley of lost species. Notable in this regard is the sandhill crane, the curlew, the greater yellow-legs and the upland plover. Fortunately, the Wilson or jacksnipe and the woodcock are still on the hunter's list of legal game. Both of these birds offer great sport afield, and they are superior as a table delicacy.

As to the care of these birds in the field, see the care of upland game birds, pages 50-51.

Plucking and Cleaning Waterfowl

In making the final preparations before cooking, the following suggestions are offered: Shallow-water or pond ducks, such as the mallard, teals or pintail, are easier to pluck than the deepwater, or sea and bay ducks such as the canvasback, redhead, or scaups. However, both ducks and geese can be plucked easier when they are warm, but the job isn't a difficult one even after they have cooled out. Lay the bird on its back in your left hand with the head and neck folded underneath between its back and the palm of your hand. Hook your thumb over the wing close to the body, and the forefinger in a like manner over the opposite wing; pull the wings back in a hammerlock fashion; this leaves the breast free. The bird may be held firmly on your knee, or, if it is a large bird, between your knees; point the front away from you. Now, with your right thumb and forefinger, grasp a small patch of the breast feathers firmly and, with a short quick jerk directed against the lay of the feathers, pluck. Only a little of the down will come off with the feathers and, after finishing the breast, remove the balance of the down by rubbing upward or against the lay with the ball of your thumb and the heel of your palm.

The back is plucked the same as the breast, except that the head and neck are folded over and along the breast instead of along the back of the bird.

To remove the pinfeathers, grasp them between your thumb and the point of a knife and pluck backward and upward from the trend. Singe well over an open flame and remove the oil sac and cut off the head. Slip the neck skin back over the neck bone without breaking the skin and sever the neck close to the body. Remove the gullet and trachea or windpipe. If the bird is bloody inside because of shot wounds, wash it in cold water, but don't soak it; wipe dry with a cloth and hang in a dry drafty place for a day or two before cooking.

Part IX

Waterfowl and Shore Bird Cookery

Because the average waterfowl gunner has little or no information about the ducks he bags, wild duck has the reputation of being something less than good table fare. This, however, is unfortunate, because quite the contrary is true, for canvasback, redhead, scaups, mallard, black duck, pintail, and the teals are all excellent and, when they are properly cared for and prepared as they should be, they are delightful food. And so, we offer here simple but reliable methods for preparing these ducks for the table.

Before preparing any of the recipes suggested for waterfowl, check pages 64-65 on cleaning these birds.

Since the epicure has bestowed upon the canvasback the honor of being the "King of Ducks," and, because we agree, we begin these recipes with His Majesty, "Canard Cheval," as he is known in Louisiana.

Roasted Canvasback Duck

Prepare the required number of ducks, being careful to

wipe them perfectly dry with a clean cloth. Season inside with a pinch of salt and a little freshly crushed black pepper. Tie the neck skin firmly, sew up the vent opening, and brush over with oil. Place the birds, breast up, in a dry roasting pan and put in a 500⁰ oven, without covering, for 18 minutes; baste occasionally with a little melted butter and the juice of 1 lemon. When the birds have roasted for 18 minutes, reduce the heat to moderate, season the outside of the birds with salt and pepper, turn breast down, cover, and continue to roast for 20 minutes, or a little longer, if the birds are old.

To serve, place the ducks in the center of a hot platter, garnish with the required number of oyster canapés (see recipe for Oyster Garnish, page 113), and send to the table with a tossed green salad.

Broiled Canvasback Duck

Select young birds, split down the back, break the wishbone and flatten. Wipe thoroughly dry with a cloth, season with a pinch of salt, brush with oil, and sear over hot coals on the brazier or open grill. Reduce the heat and broil for about 15 or 18 more minutes to the side. Baste frequently with a mixture of 1 part melted butter and 2 parts orange juice.

To serve, place the birds in the center of a hot dish and surround with slices of fried hominy grits. Sprinkle over all chopped parsley and freshly crushed black pepper.

Broiled Redhead Duck

See above recipe.

Roasted Mallard With Wild Rice

Select two mallards, clean, rub inside with a little salt and crushed black pepper, sew up both ends and brush with oil. Sear well for 10 minutes in a brisk oven and finish roasting in a moderate oven until tender — about 45 minutes. Five minutes before serving, season outside with salt and crushed black pepper.

To serve, place the birds four inches apart in the center of a hot dish, heap wild rice between them, and decorate with watercress.

Wild Rice

Allow ½ cup dry rice for each duck; wash well and soak in cold water for several hours, or overnight. Drain and put into an abundance of boiling salted water, without covering. Boiling time should take about 10 or 12 minutes. (Be sure the rice is tender but not overcooked.) Rinse by pouring copious quantities of cold water over it; drain in a colander, and, when thoroughly drained and fluffy, sauté in butter in a large heavy frypan. Turn continually with a spatula, and shake the pan occasionally to keep the rice from sticking.

Teal Ducks in Casserole

Clean carefully four teal ducks, season inside with a little salt and crushed black pepper, brush over with oil and roast in a brisk oven for 15 minutes.

Put 2 tablespoons melted butter in a large deep frypan; when hot, add 1 medium-sized diced onion, 1 diced carrot, 2 sticks chopped celery, and ½ cup chopped mushrooms. Turn and stir with a spatula until half done, or for about 6 minutes. Now add 3 tablespoons sherry and the juice of ½ lemon. Blend well and season with salt and pepper, put in a casserole, place the ducks on top, cover and cook in moderate oven for 30 minutes.

To serve, place the vegetables on a hot dish, top with the ducks, and send to the table.

Pintail Duck With Brandy

Prepare three pintail ducks, wipe dry and season with

salt and black pepper, brush with oil, and roast in a brisk oven for 18 minutes to each side.

While the ducks are roasting, put 1 small diced onion, 1 bay leaf, pinch nutmeg, 6 whole peppercorns, and ½ cup red wine in a frypan. Place over very slow fire and allow to simmer 6 or 8 minutes.

Now take the roasted ducks and carve all of the meat from the bones; slice the breast in ¼-inch thick slices. Arrange the pieces of duck in a casserole and pour ½ cup warm brandy over them, and set alight. When it has burned out, add 2 tablespoons good stock or 1 tablespoon hot water, and 1 tablespoon melted butter, cover tightly and set aside in a warm place.

Break and pound the carcasses from which the flesh was carved, add them to the onions and stock, or hot water, cover, and let simmer for 30 minutes. Just before serving, strain this stock over the ducks that are in the casserole; add 1 cup quartered mushrooms that have been cooked in a little butter, and return to a moderate oven for 5 or 6 minutes; then serve.

Braised Scaup Duck With Cabbage

The scaup ducks, both the greater and the lesser species, are generally quite fat, and this fat ofttimes imparts a strong "ducky" flavor to the flesh of the roasted bird. It is, therefore, wise to season them well and to serve them with vegetables. Thus, we offer "Duck With Cabbage."

Clean, singe and wipe thoroughly dry three ducks. Place breast up in a dry roasting pan; leave uncovered, and roast in a brisk oven for 25 minutes. Remove from the roaster, pour off the grease that has accumulated in the bottom of the pan, rinse the pan, and return the ducks, breast down.

Into a frypan put 2 tablespoons melted butter and 1 rounded tablespoon flour; cream into a smooth paste over a slow fire and add 1½ cups good stock or hot water. Season with salt and crushed black pepper, 1 small bay leaf, and a sprig of parsley. Let simmer 5 minutes, then pour over the ducks in the roaster, cover and cook in a moderate oven for 30 minutes, or until tender.

While the ducks are braising, take 1 small head of cabbage (preferably the red variety) that weighs about 1½ pounds. Shred coarsely and cook in just enough salted water to keep it from sticking. When almost tender, sprinkle over it 2 teaspoons sugar and 2 tablespoons vinegar. Cover and continue to cook until slightly underdone. Remove the cabbage and drain off all of the broth from it, in case there is any left; turn into a frypan and cook in a little butter until slightly browned.

To serve, heap the cabbage in the center of a hot dish, and top with the ducks. Now skim the contents that is left in the bottom of the pan of all grease before pouring it over the ducks.

Duck With Turnips

Prepare two ducks for roasting (pintails, mallards, gadwalls, or other species may be used). Sear to a golden brown over a bed of coals or in a hot oven. If the birds are seared in the oven, drain off all of the grease and rinse the pan before adding butter or oil.

Now put 3 tablespoons melted butter or cooking oil into the roasting pan; when hot, add 1½ tablespoons flour and cream to a smooth paste, then dilute with 2 cups good poultry or beef stock; stir continually until thoroughly blended. Season the ducks with salt and pepper, place them breast down in the roasting pan, baste with the sauce, cover tightly, and cook in moderate oven 25 minutes.

While the ducks are roasting, peel and pare just a little over 1 pound of firm sweet turnips and cut them into round, ½-inch thick slices. Put in a frypan with just enough butter or oil to keep them from sticking, and sauté to a light brown. Season with salt and 2 teaspoons sugar.

71

When they have browned, add them to the ducks, cover again, and roast slowly for 40 minutes longer.

To serve, put the ducks in the center of a hot dish, surround with the turnips, and strain the gravy over all.

Salmi of Coot

Skin, clean, and wipe dry the breasts of four coots; season with salt and crushed black pepper and brush with oil. Sear over bright coals or in a brisk oven, then place in a roasting pan, pour over them 1 cup hot stock, cover and braise slowly.

Put ½ cup diced ham or bacon, 1 diced carrot, 1 chopped onion, 1 small minced clove garlic and a little nutmeg in a frypan. Cook over a slow fire for 10 minutes, stirring and turning with a spatula. Now add this to the coots in the roaster, cover again, and simmer until all is quite tender.

To serve, place the coot breasts in the center of a hot dish and pour the sauce over them.

Roasted Goose With Apples

Peel and core 5 or 6 apples; put 1 slight teaspoon brown sugar (granulated may be substituted), and 1 whole clove where the core was removed.

Singe, clean and wipe dry a young goose. Rub inside with salt and pepper, stuff with the cored apples, sew up both ends, truss, brush with oil and place breast up in a roasting pan. Sear in a hot oven for 20 minutes, then turn breast down, season with salt and pepper, cover tightly, reduce heat to moderate, and roast 1½ or 2 hours, or until tender. Baste occasionally with the broth which accumulates in the pan.

Put the giblets in a saucepan, season with salt, cover with boiling water, and simmer until tender, then mince them fine and add, along with the broth in which they were cooked, to the gravy which is prepared when the goose has roasted long enough.

Now remove the goose from the roasting pan; skim off all fat from the broth; cream 2 tablespoons flour and 2 tablespoons melted butter to a smooth paste; add to the broth and, if it thickens too much, add hot stock or boiling water. Add the minced giblets, season with salt and pepper, and serve in a gravy boat.

Place the goose on a hot platter, garnish with the apples that it was stuffed with, and browned new potatoes.

Goose in Sauce

Singe and clean the bird and put it in a large kettle with the giblets; cover with slightly salted boiling water, bring to a boil and skim carefully. Now add 2 medium-sized sliced onions, 3 sliced carrots, 1 sprig parsley, 1 bay leaf, a few celery leaves, 4 cloves and 8 whole peppercorns. Simmer slowly until the goose is tender, then remove it from the kettle and carve all of the meat from the carcass. Put several tablespoons melted butter or oil in a large frypan; when hot, brown the pieces of goose lightly, then cover with the following sauce.

Into a saucepan put 3 cups milk and 5 small whole cloves garlic; simmer gently until garlic is tender, then remove it from the milk. Toast 4 slices whole wheat bread, crumble rather fine, then add to the hot milk. When bread is well blended, strain the sauce through a colander or a sieve into another saucepan. Now beat 4 egg yolks, blend into them ½ cup cream and 4 tablespoons of the hot milk in which the garlic was cooked, and add this to the bread crumbs and the rest of the milk. Place over a slow fire and simmer for a few minutes, stirring continually. When all the ingredients are thoroughly blended, pour the sauce over the slices of goose, and serve.

As to the shore birds, they are so much alike that they

can all be prepared for the table in the same manner. However, we offer two recipes for woodcock, both of which may be used for any of the other shore birds. In addition to these recipes, these birds respond equally well to frying in deep fat, roasting and braising. See recipes for the small upland game birds, pages 53-62.

Camp Broiled Woodcock

Singe, clean and wipe thoroughly dry the required number of birds (see pages 50-51 on cleaning upland game birds). Split down the back and flatten; brush with oil or lard; place on a brazier or open grill, either at home or in camp, and sear well over hot coals, then finish broiling over moderate heat, allowing 5 or 6 minutes to the side.

When cleaning the giblets be sure to remove the gall bladder from the livers. Mince the giblets fine and add to them 1 rounding tablespoon finely chopped onion; put all in a frypan with 1 tablespoon melted butter and cook over a slow fire until onions are tender but not browned. Now add 1 heaping teaspoon flour; when thoroughly blended, moisten with just enough hot water to make a soft paste. Season with salt and freshly crushed black pepper.

For each bird, cut pieces of bread 2 inches wide and 3 inches long, then toast; spread the toast with the onion and liver paste and top with the birds. Season the birds with salt and crushed pepper and dash over them a little melted butter.

Broiled Woodcock With Bacon

Prepare and broil the birds as in the preceding recipe; arrange on a hot dish and garnish each bird with a slice of broiled bacon.

Part X

The Fishes

There are many, many species of edible fishes that inhabit the sea and our inland waters. Some of them are more delicious than others; some are abundant; and some have suffered depletion in numbers because of heavy fishing or pollution. Using scientific methods of propagation and restoration, the federal and state agencies who deal in such matters are striving frantically to keep abreast with the ever increasing demands upon the fishery resources of the country by both the sportsman and the commercial fisherman. The job is a most difficult one, especially with our inland waters where the denudation of soil and subsequent erosion have accelerated the deterioration of the waters and contributed to the progressive decline in their productivity of fishery crops. It is a sad and unresolved problem which time, we hope, will take care of.

Care of Fish

Keeping a catch of fish in good condition for one or

more days without ice is a problem. Game improves with curing and aging but this is definitely not the case with fish for they are extremely perishable; and the species with the most delicate flavor are more susceptible to deterioration than those that are coarse and strong in flavor. Most of our fishing is done in the spring, summer and early autumn when the weather ranges from warm to hot and humid, especially at low altitudes. Today, the icebox is usually a part of the fisherman's equipment, but inasmuch as it prevents the proper air circulation, fish that are held for too long in the stale and subsequently foul air, deteriorate considerably. So, it might be well to offer the following suggestions.

Fish should be killed and drawn as soon as possible. Remove the gills and the kidney (which lies in the back of the cavity), and wipe dry with a cloth, grass, or leaves.

If it can be avoided, never leave fish on a stringer or in a live-box for a long period. Fish, especially the game species, are nervous and excitable creatures and holding them alive under abnormal conditions is decidedly detrimental. This is because secretions from the endocrine glands of a frightened, nervous, or angry creature flow into the blood or lymph and contaminate the flesh.

Never let fish touch while they are in the creel. This is especially true of trout. After drawing, wipe dry and keep separated with dry, not green, grass which will allow the air to circulate through the creel. If fish are piled one on top of the other and are wet with slime and water, they will soften and deteriorate rapidly.

Fish should not be put in water to keep them fresh, regardless of the water's low temperature; nor should they be left in the sun, for they will soften rapidly and lose much of their flavor.

Unless they are to be kept for a long time, fish should not be frozen. Most foods suffer from freezing but this is particularly true of fish for their flesh is more flaky than other meats and in thawing the juices escape more rapidly

76

and, with the loss of the juices, the deliciousness of the fish suffers. Chowders, gumbos, bisques, and similar dishes may be prepared with greater success while the fish are still frozen, since the juices escape into the broth.

Never dress fish and soak for hours in brine or vinegar unless you want salted or pickled fish. This practice of soaking fish in some sort of solution on the theory that it improves the flavor or extracts some objectionable taste, is not only illogical but detrimental to fish cookery. The mossy or rotten log taint often found in the flesh of fresh-water fishes is caused by moldlike microorganisms which are known as actinomyces which exist in mud, decaying vegetation and water, during periods of hot weather and low water. These microorganisms are taken into the blood stream through the gills then into the tissues of the fish, which produces an unsavory taint which remains in spite of soaking, seasoning or other culinary treatment.

Heat, rain and subsequent humidity, which usually occur at low altitudes, cause rapid deterioration not only of fish and game, but of any perishable food, for that matter, and such foods should not be held more than a few hours without ice. The cool, dry, rarefied air at high altitudes reduces bacteria greatly and thus retards putre-faction. Under such conditions, fish may be held without ice for a longer period, provided they are killed, drawn and wiped dry immediately.

Cleaning Fish

There are many anglers and housewives who succeed in doing a rather miserable job of cleaning fish. There is, however, little necessity for bungling this simple operation if, as is the case in anything else, one approaches the job with some understanding and is diligent enough to acquire some skill.

Bones and more bones seem to be the woe of the average fish eater, and it isn't uncommon to find those who

77

deny themselves the pleasure of eating fish simply because they actually fear the bones, which is unfortunate and unnecessary. It is possible, in most instances, to reduce the hazard of getting a bone if care is taken when the fish are cleaned.

First of all, if we are to learn the best methods for cleaning fish, a knowledge of the skeletal structure of the more familiar species is of great importance. This knowledge isn't difficult to obtain for a little well directed observation is all that is needed. For example, it is a rather simple matter to divide the more familiar fresh-water species into their respective groups or families. Clarify these groups in your mind; study the skeletal structure of a single member of each group and you will have the key to the skeletal structure of the entire group.

Say, for instance, we study the vast family of sunfishes which includes the crappies, the black basses, the rock bass, the bluegill, and many others. Besides the fins and the bones supporting the pectorals and ventral fins (which can be cut away easily), the bones of these fishes include the backbone or vertebrae, the ribs, and a row of small bones that are attached to the ribs on either side and extend the length of the visceral cavity.

As a whole, there is little difference between the skeletal structure of the sunfishes and the family to which the walleyed pike, the yellow perch, and other species belong. The same may be said of the family to which the fresh-water white bass belongs. However, the true pikes (muskellunge, northern pike and pickerels) are different in that they have small floating bifurcated bones which are located between the back muscles. Other than the bones which support the fins and the spines, the catfishes have only the vertebrae and rib bones.

If objectionable bones are to be avoided, fish must be filleted. To me, this method of preparing fish is not only the easiest but the most satisfactory; but it is here that a knowledge of the skeletal structure is important. The job of filleting isn't a difficult one, and a little practice will perfect your skill.

Let's take the fillets from a two-pound bass. Lay the fish on a board or any flat surface, with the tail pointing away from you and the dorsal or back fin pointing to the right. Hold the fish by pressing the left hand firmly on the head and upper portion of the body. With a short-bladed knife, cut along the upper side of the body from the bottom of the dorsal fin to the base of the skull; slant the blade so as to follow the fin bones and the back down to the top of the ribs. Repeat the operation on the opposite side. Make a like incision, which will be much shorter, on each side of the anal fin from the vent to the tail. Turn the fish across at right angles to you, slant the knife and cut under each pectoral fin just back of the gill opening; don't sever the head. Return the fish to the original position and, with the left thumb, open the incision along the dorsal fin; with the knife blade following the outer edge of the ribs, cut the fillet free down to the belly line. Then, with the knife blade following the backbone, slice the fillet free from the bone from the vent down to the tail. Repeat this operation on the other side. Scaling the fish is unnecessary if it weighs as much as one pound. Furthermore, if you clean it shortly after catching, drawing is also unnecessary; the fillets can be taken off without any other operation.

When the fillets have been removed, the skin can be taken off of each piece by loosening the edge at the tail end with the point of the knife. Grasp the skin with the thumbnail and the edge of the forefinger and, with the knife blade slanting toward the inside of the skin, simply peel the flesh from the skin. The only bones left in the fillet will be the small ones along the lateral line for the length of the visceral cavity and a portion of the shoulder girder that supports the pectoral fin. These can be removed easily with the point of the knife.

The fillets of fish that are less than one pound are best with the skin left on because the strips of flesh are small and thin and the skin helps to hold them in shape. These smaller fish should be scaled first and boned as directed above.

It is best to leave trout whole, unless the fish weighs two or three pounds, when it can be boned as directed. Because trout bones are soft and pliable they aren't as difficult to cope with when eating as are the spiny-finned fishes. When small fish, such as pan-sized trout, are cleaned to be served whole, a simple way to draw them is to cut the isthmus or throat, free the gills from the body and draw out all of the intestines with the gills; cut out the vent.

When drawing fish in this manner it isn't necessary to slit the belly. Too, when such fish as smelt are taken, especially when they are running and are ripe with spawn, the fish may be cleaned with the roe left intact in the visceral cavity which makes it possible to cook the roe with the fish.

The catfishes have no scales and they must be skinned. These fishes hold tenaciously to life and it is necessary to kill them before cleaning. The most effective way to do this is to slip the point of a knife into the small opening in the skull which is directly in the center of the head on a line slightly back of the eyes; slip a broom or grass straw at an angle so that the straw will run down the spinal cord toward the tail. Be sure to grasp the fish firmly and be careful to avoid the sharp spines when it writhes from the death shock as the straw punctures the spinal cord.

To skin a catfish, cut through the skin under each pectoral spine, around the nape of the neck on both sides of the dorsal spine and down the back to the tail. Take care not to cut too deeply into the flesh but only through the skin. Don't cut the skin across the fish's throat. Now peel a flap of the skin back on each side of the dorsal spine at the nape of the neck and, if the fish is small, catch this flap of skin between the thumb and the knife blade and pull outward and downward toward the tail. It is best

80

to use small, flat-nosed pliers if the fish is large. There will be a V-shaped piece of skin on the belly which can be peeled off by catching at the point of the V just above the vent; pull this upward toward the head. After skinning, split the belly from the vent to the throat, strip the intestines from the vent toward the head and break the head back and sever the spine at the neck. The intestines will come with the head. If desired, fillets from catfish may be taken after the fish has been skinned, in which case, directions for filleting bass should be followed.

If small fish such as perch, crappie, bluegill, etc. are to be cooked whole, they should be drawn and scaled; the back or dorsal and the anal or belly fins should be removed entirely. To do this, cut on each side of the fin and grasp it at the bottom with the thumb and knife blade, pull outward and upward and jerk the whole fin out by the roots.

Terrapins

Tortoises, terrapins, and turtles are often confused and it might help to clarify this confusion if we point out that the tortoises are land dwellers; the terrapins inhabit fresh water; and the huge green turtle of the sea is the best example of the marine turtles. However, the soft-shelled terrapin is our immediate concern, for, contrary to the accepted opinion, it is clean in its food habits and the meat is delicate in flavor. In truth, those who have never eaten terrapin soup when it was properly prepared, have missed a great treat.

Cleaning Terrapins

To the inexperienced, dressing a terrapin looks difficult but, actually, the job is quite simple. Say we start with the soft-shelled. First, cut the head off and let the terrapin bleed freely. Although decapitating won't cause immediate death, it will come in a short time. Now, turn the terrapin on its back and cut around each leg, the tail and the neck with a sharp knife; cut through the cartilaginous seam on each side which connects the plastron or lower portion of the shell with the carapace or upper portion; peel off the lower plate and dissect the forelegs, the neck, and the hind legs with the pelvic arch and tail from the upper shell. (If the terrapin is a female and ripe with eggs, you may smile on your good fortune for the eggs are an especial delicacy.) When the legs have been dissected from the shell, split the skin down to the claws and pull it from the meat with pliers.

There are two methods for cleaning the hard-shelled turtles (the snappers). One method is to use a camp ax or butcher's cleaver to break the plastron or belly plate from the shell; the meat can then be removed the same as it is when the soft-shelled terrapin is cleaned.

The other method is to cut off the head and hang the turtle neck down until the blood stops dripping. Wash well in cold water and then drop into a kettle of boiling water for 10 or 15 minutes. Now pour off the water and cover the turtle with cold water and let stand until cool enough to handle; with a dry cloth, rub off the dark epidermis from the skin on the legs and remove the claws. Return the turtle to the kettle of water and continue boiling for 40 minutes to an hour, depending upon its size and age. When the skin of the legs is jellylike, remove the turtle from the kettle; let it cool enough to handle easily; place it on its back and remove the belly plate and the skin from the legs and neck; take the meat out of the upper shell. Save the eggs, if there are any, and add them to the meat. The pieces of turtle are now ready to use in any dish you wish to prepare.

Frogs

In the European and Latin American countries, the flesh of frogs has long been regarded as a real delicacy and, more recently, its popularity has increased in the United States. The most valuable species is the giant bullfrog, however, the hind legs of the common or green frog are edible.

Cleaning Frogs

To clean, make a crosswise incision just through the skin midway on the back; slip the fingers of each hand into this incision and pull in opposite directions simultaneously. If the frogs are small, as is the case with the common frog, skin with the aid of a small pair of pliers.

After removing the skin, draw, cut off the head, and trim the feet. Save all of the bullfrog, but only the hindquarters of the smaller species.

Part XI

Fish Cookery

When passing judgment upon the goodness of any species of fish it is necessary to consider the factors which contribute to or take from their goodness. To begin with, fish must be prime and to be prime they must be taken from water which contributes the most to the habitat requirements of a particular species, i.e. temperature, mineral and oxygen content, bottom type, kind and quantity of food present, and other ecologic factors. Second, the care of the fish from the time it is taken until it reaches the cook must be considered. And third, the method employed in preparing the fish for the table must not be overlooked, for it is most important to remember that all species of fish fail to respond equally well to the same culinary treatment. For example, there is a vast difference between the way the whitefishes and the catfishes are prepared, i.e. the whitefishes are primarily broiling fishes and the catfishes are best when they are fried in deep hot fat. And it would be a travesty to reverse this order of preparation for

85

to fry a whitefish would mean destroying its delicate flavor and to broil a catfish would be unheard of. And so, there is definitely a right way to cook the various species, and recognition of and adhering to this fact will add to the delight in eating any fish.

No matter where we go, either in America or in other lands, we will encounter definite food habits and preferences which have been a part of a culture for generations, and it would, therefore, not only be presumptuous but foolhardy to suggest changes in any method of cookery. With this in mind, we offer our experience in preparing fish for the table.

The Whitefishes

Of the several species of whitefishes, which, on the whole, are restricted to the Great Lakes region and some of the larger lakes of the United States and Canada, the common whitefish is doubtless the most important of the group. However, pollution is a serious threat to all of the species' survival.

Broiled Whitefish

As we have stated, the whitefish should always be broiled and, inasmuch as a bed of hardwood coals is unequalled for this method of cooking, we offer camp broiled whitefish as the *piece de résistance* of all fish dishes. If, however, you have a brazier, or an open grate in the backyard, or on the patio, your problem for broiling this fish at home is solved.

Select a fish that weighs 2 or 3 pounds; scale, draw, fillet and wipe dry. (See pages 77-81 on cleaning fish.) Brush with oil and lay on a double wire broiler. Hold the flesh side near the bed of glowing coals and broil for 15 or 18 minutes, turn and broil on the skin side for 3 minutes. Remove from the broiler and place in the center of a heated dish; season with salt and a little black pepper, dash with melted butter and garnish with wedges of lemon and send to the table.

Serve with this dish new potatoes that have been boiled in their jackets, peeled, heated in browned butter and sprinkled with chopped parsley. A tossed green salad also compliments this dish.

The Shad

There are several species of shads and all of them are related to the herrings. Like the salmons, they are anadromous fishes; that is, they spend most of their life in the sea and run up the rivers to spawn.

The finest species of the group and definitely the one of greatest importance as a food fish, is the common or American shad. So delicious is the flavor of the fresh shad that I'm sure there are those who will challenge the right of the whitefish to head this list of fine food fishes.

The shad, however, possesses the maximum number of bones to the cubic inch. Even so, unless one has an irrepressible phobia regarding fishbones, the exquisite flavor and the juicy, fine-grained flesh of this fish will more than compensate for dealing with this objectionable feature.

Broiled Shad

Follow the recipe for broiling whitefish, unless the fish contains roe, in which case, wash and wipe it dry, season with salt and pepper, brush with oil and broil, allowing 6 minutes to the side.

Grill or broil 6 slices of bacon and when the fish is ready to serve put it in the center of a hot dish, garnish with the grilled bacon, broiled roe, and 6 wedges of lemon; dash 4 tablespoons melted butter over all, and send to the table piping hot.

87

Planked Shad

Scale, draw and remove the fins, head and tail from a 2-pound shad. If there is roe, leave it inside the fish. Score crosswise three times on each side. Season both inside and out with salt and pepper, baste with oil, and let stand for 5 minutes. Arrange on a plank or cast aluminum broiler plate, and put to broil for 20 minutes.

Just before the fish is ready to serve, encircle it with potatoes that have been whipped with butter and cream; return to the broiler and cook until the potatoes are slightly browned on top. Remove from the broiler, dash 2 tablespoons melted butter over the fish, garnish with wedges of lemon, sprinkle a little chopped parsley over the potatoes, and serve.

The Smelts

Like the whitefishes, the smelts are distantly related to the salmons and trouts, they are numerous, and they have a most delicate and delightful flavor. In truth, the name itself comes from the fact that when these little fishes are absolutely fresh they have an odor that has been compared to freshly sliced cucumbers, wild flowers and dew-wet ferns. But this fragrance is so fragile that it is destroyed if the fish is frozen or stored for any length of time.

The Eulachon, a related species, is often referred to as the candlefish. This stems from the fact that they are so oily that the Indians used to dry them, place a wick in their tails and use them as candles.

Fried Smelts

Select the required number of smelts and wipe perfectly dry with a clean cloth (the scales may be removed with this operation). Draw and leave the heads intact; dip in milk, season with salt and pepper, and roll in flour.

Have boiling hot fat in a deep frypan, drop the fish into it, and cook for about 3 minutes, or until they are a golden brown. Be sure that the fat is absolutely sweet, otherwise it will destroy the fishes' exquisite flavor.

Smelts With Wine

Prepare the fish the same as for frying, except for cutting off the heads. With a sharp knife, slit down the back and remove the backbone, then press each fish together again. In a large fry or saucepan heat 3 tablespoons butter to moderately hot, then carefully add the fish. Season with salt and black pepper and cook for 2 minutes; turn with a spatula, and repeat this process. Pour over them 1 small glass white wine, then add 1 cup chopped mushrooms with the liquid in which they were cooked, and cook for about 4 minutes or until the moisture is reduced by half.

To serve, arrange the fish on a hot dish, pour the sauce over them, and decorate with a little water cress.

Broiled Smelts

See recipe for broiled whitefish.

Smelts Au Gratin

Prepare the smelts the same as for broiling. Put 1 tablespoon melted butter in a baking dish; lay in the fish, season with salt and pepper and sprinkle with 3 tablespoons white wine; dust a few fresh bread crumbs over the top, dot with butter, and put in a hot oven for 10 or 12 minutes.

Before serving, sprinkle 1 teaspoon chopped parsley over the top and send to the table with a few slices of lemon.

The Lake Trout

The lake trout, which is known by many other names,

such as Mackinaw trout, togue trout, lake salmon, and siscowet, is an inhabitant of the deep cold lakes of the northern United States, Canada, and Alaska. It is the largest of all of the trouts, occasionally attaining a weight of close to 100 pounds. While it may be considered an angler's fish, since it is taken with the trolling spoon, and, at times, on the fly, it is chiefly important to the commercial fishermen. The flesh of this fish is fine grained, juicy and most delicate in flavor.

Broiled Lake Trout

See recipe for broiled whitefish.

Baked Lake Trout

Draw, scale and remove the fins from a 4-pound fish. Wipe dry with a clean cloth, score each side crosswise three times, season inside and out with salt and pepper, and brush with oil. Put 2 tablespoons melted butter into a roasting pan, lay in the fish, pour over it a glass of white wine, 1 cup chopped mushrooms with the liquid in which they were cooked, and cover well with aluminum foil; place in a moderate oven and bake for 45 minutes, or until fish is tender and flaky, but firm.

Put the fish in the center of a hot dish, pour the mushrooms and the liquid over it, garnish with quartered fresh tomatoes, wedges of lemon, and send to the table.

Poached Lake Trout

Scale and wipe dry a 3-pound trout, then fillet. Fill a flat shallow saucepan (that is large enough to accommodate the fillets without folding them) with boiling salted water, to which has been added ½ cup vinegar, 1 small sliced onion, 1 sliced and diced carrot, and 6 whole peppercorns. Gently lay the pieces of trout into the water and let them boil slowly for about 15 minutes, or until they are tender, but still quite firm. Carefully lift the fillets from the water, drain well, and arrange in the center of a hot dish.

Serve with Egg Sauce (see sauce recipes), sprinkle with chopped parsley, and garnish with boiled potatoes.

Sauteed Fillets of Lake Trout

Select fish that weigh about 2 pounds, scale, wipe dry, and fillet. Dip in milk, season with salt and pepper, roll lightly in flour and sauté in butter or oil. Turn frequently, and be sure the fat holds a temperature that will not burn the fillets. When they are a golden brown, place them on a hot dish, garnish with quartered fresh tomatoes and sliced cucumbers, sprinkle with a little chopped parsley, and serve with wedges of lemon.

Other Species of Trouts

Although all of the trouts are superior table fishes and are highly prized by the angler, for me, at least, the brook is the prince of the clan. Little wonder that this beautiful fish has for centuries been the subject of song, poetry, and story.

Other species of the native and introduced trouts that are well known are the rainbow, cutthroat, Dolly Varden, German brown and Loch Leven.

The flesh of the trouts is not dissimilar and the recipes offered here work equally well for all.

Broiled Trout

See recipe for broiled whitefish.

Sauteed Trout

See recipe for sautéed lake trout.

Trout in Egg Sauce

Clean, wash and dry trout that weigh about ½ pound each. Season inside and out with salt and pepper, put in a well-buttered baking dish and then in a hot oven for 15 minutes.

Now prepare the Egg Sauce. (See sauce recipes.)

To serve, place the trout on a hot dish, pour the sauce over them, and sprinkle with chopped parsley.

Trout in Shrimp Sauce

Follow the above recipe but serve with Shrimp Sauce instead of Egg Sauce. (See sauce recipes.)

Fried Trout

As a rule, trout should not be fried in deep fat, but small fish are not too bad when prepared in this manner. Select only small trout, dip in milk, season with salt and pepper, roll in flour or corn meal and cook to a golden brown in deep boiling fat. Be sure the fat is sweet, otherwise the flavor of the fish will suffer. When the fish are done, lift them from the fat and drain on paper.

Serve on a hot dish and surround with new boiled potatoes or plain boiled rice and sliced tomatoes.

Trout on the Stream

Ofttimes, when the entire day is spent on the trout stream, it is good to take time at noon to stop for a spell to have lunch, to smoke a pipe, and to view the hills down the skyline. In anticipation of this, before leaving camp, remember to put in your fishing jacket pocket a butter-and-bread sandwich, 1 or 2 slices of bacon, an apple, a potato that has been boiled in its jacket, and a pinch of salt and pepper.

Form a small tepee of hardwood sticks, kindle, and,

while the fire is burning down to a bed of bright coals, select the desired number of small trout, draw and wipe dry with alder leaves. Cut a green sweetwood twig for each trout; season the fish with salt and pepper, skewer to each one a piece of bacon, impale on the green twigs, and broil over the coals.

If several trout are to be broiled, sharpen the large end of the twigs and stick them in the ground at an angle so that the trout lean against or above the coals. Turn occasionally to insure even broiling. It will take from 4 to 5 minutes.

Cut two more twigs, peel and cut the potato in half, season with salt and pepper, impale on the twigs, and roast over the coals.

Spread the paper in which the bread was wrapped on a flat stone and when the food is ready lay it on the paper.

The Intermediate Fishes

Intermediate between the cold water and the warm water fishes are the true pikes and the perches. And the walleyed pike, or pike perch, is one of America's finest food fishes, and it is equally important both as a commercial fish and an angler's fish. It is often called jack salmon in its southern range, and it inhabits the clear waters of the lakes and streams of the Mississippi Valley from Arkansas, north into Canada, and eastward into New York State. It sometimes attains a weight of 20 pounds, but a fish weighing 5 or 6 pounds is considered a good specimen.

Walleyed Pike Fried in Deep Fat

Fillet the required number of fish. If large fish are selected, the thicker portions of the fillets should be split so as to be not more than 1 inch thick. Have frying fat boiling hot in a deep fry kettle. Dip the fillets in milk, season with salt and pepper, roll in either flour, corn meal

93

or cracker dust, and fry to a rich brown. Lift from the fat and drain well. Arrange in the center of a hot dish, decorate with wedges of lemon and serve.

Fillets of Walleyed Pike Sauteed in Butter

Prepare the fish as in the preceding recipe, and sauté in hot butter over a moderate fire, taking care not to let the butter burn. Turn occasionally with a spatula. When the fillets are a light brown, arrange them on a hot dish, pour melted butter over them, sprinkle with chopped parsley and serve.

The abundant, and justly famous yellow perch, and the sauger, or sand pike, are related to the walleyed pike. These fishes are not unlike the walleyed pike and they can be prepared in the same manner.

The True Pikes

The pikes include the pickerels, the great northern pike, and the muskellunges. Although these fishes are thought of primarily as sport fishes, the flesh is firm, flaky and quite good when they are taken from clean, cold water. However, they are very bony, which does not contribute to the pleasure in eating them.

The pikes may be fried (see any of the recipes suggested for frying other fish), but if variety is desired in their preparation, we offer the following.

Fillet of Pike Au Gratin

Cut the fillets into individual servings; brush them lightly with melted butter or cooking oil, and place in a well-greased, flat baking pan.

Into 2 tablespoons heated butter, cream to a smooth paste 1 tablespoon flour; add 1 cup chicken stock or hot

94

water and blend thoroughly. Then add 1 heaping table-spoon finely chopped onion, the juice of half a lemon, 1 sprig finely chopped parsley and salt and pepper to season. Let simmer for 2 minutes, stirring continually to prevent sticking, and pour over the fish. Sprinkle bread crumbs over the top and bake in a 450° oven for 20 or 25 minutes.

Serve piping hot with plain buttered rice and a green salad.

Baked Pike With Stuffing

Select a 4- or 5-pound fish; draw, scale, remove the head, tail, and fins, wash in cold water and wipe dry. Season inside with salt and pepper and stuff with the following:

Brown 1 small onion very lightly in 4 tablespoons melted butter and add to 1½ cups crumbled bread; season with salt and pepper, bind with 1 lightly beaten egg and stuff the fish. Sew or skewer the fish, score crosswise four times on the upper side, lay in a well-greased baking pan, strip with 3 slices bacon, and put to bake in a 400° oven for 10 minutes; reduce the heat to 300° and continue to bake for 30 or 40 minutes, according to the size of the fish. Serve on a hot platter; garnish with sliced tomatoes. A green salad and Tartar Sauce compliment this dish. (See sauce recipes.)

The Sunfishes

This group of fishes includes many of the better known species that are of interest to the angler. They are abundant and are distributed over a wide range of this continent. The most important members of the group are the black basses — the smallmouth or bronzeback, the spotted small-mouth, and the largemouth. Following the basses are the two species of crappies — the black crappie or calico bass, and the white crappie. Other species include the rock bass, bluegill, long-eared sunfish, green sunfish, and others.

Although frying in deep fat, or sautéing are the best methods for cooking any of the sunfishes, for the sake of variety, we offer the following recipes.

Bass With White Wine

Select a fish that weighs 3 or 4 pounds; draw, scale, remove the head, the tail, the dorsal and the anal fins. Wash well and wipe thoroughly dry. Make three or four crosswise incisions on both sides of the fish; season with salt and pepper inside and out; brush over with oil; place in a large buttered baking pan; moisten with ½ cup white wine and 4 tablespoons mushroom liquid; cover with aluminum foil and put to bake in a moderate oven for 30 to 40 minutes, depending upon the size of the fish. When it is thoroughly done, lift it from the baking pan and place on a hot dish.

Add just enough flour or cornstarch to the gravy that is left in the pan to thicken it slightly; add ½ cup chopped mushrooms that were cooked in a little butter. Simmer the gravy for 6 or 7 minutes over a moderate fire, then pour it over the fish.

To serve, sprinkle all with chopped parsley and decorate with browned new potatoes.

Bass Baked With Vegetables

Remove the fillets from two fish that weight 1½ or 2 pounds each. (The equivalent of smaller fish may be used.) Clean, wash and wipe perfectly dry. Put the fillets in a buttered baking dish, season with salt and pepper; add 2 cups canned tomatoes, 2 medium-sized sliced onions, 3 carrots cut julienne, 1 green pepper cut julienne, 3 sticks celery cut in large pieces, 1 bay leaf, and a little more salt for the vegetables. Moisten with 1 cup hot fish stock or water. Cover with aluminum foil and bake in a moderate oven for 40 minutes.

To serve, place the fish in the center of a hot dish, surround with the vegetables, and pour the pan broth over all.

Fillets of Bass Au Gratin

Put 2 tablespoons melted butter in a deep frypan; add 1 chopped onion, 1 cup mushrooms, and 1 small clove garlic that has been bruised to a paste. Cook the vegetables, without browning, until almost done.

Have ready 1½ or 2 pounds bass fillets. Put vegetables in a well-buttered baking dish, add 2 sprigs parsley; arrange the bass fillets on top, season with salt and crushed black pepper, moisten with ½ glass white wine, and bake in moderate oven for 15 minutes. Remove from the oven and sprinkle with fresh bread crumbs, dot with butter and return to the oven for 6 or 8 minutes longer.

To serve, sprinkle a little chopped parsley over the fish, decorate with wedges of lemon, and send to the table.

The Panfishes

A panfish is a small fish that is suitable for frying whole. A list of these fishes would include many species, but some of the more familiar are bluegill, rock bass, green sunfish, and yellow perch.

Although these fishes are small, because of the many bones, it is not only practical but wise to bone at least the larger specimens in this group. The fins of the smaller fish should be removed entirely. (See page 81.)

Panfish in Deep Fat

Clean and wipe thoroughly dry the required number of fish. Dip in milk, season with salt and pepper, or salt and a little ground chili, roll either in flour or corn meal and drop into deep, boiling hot fat. When rich brown, remove

97

and drain on paper. Serve with a sharp Tartar Sauce. (See sauce recipes.)

Oven-Fried Panfish

Either fillets or whole fish can be cooked in this manner. Wash the fish briefly in cold water and wipe perfectly dry. Dip in milk, season with salt and pepper, and roll in bread crumbs. Place the fish in a well-greased, flat baking pan, sprinkle with a little sweet oil or melted butter, and put in a brisk 550° oven to bake for 10 or 12 minutes, according to the size or thickness of the fish.

The Catfishes

The species of catfishes are many, and they are well distributed throughout the warm waters of the continent. Although their endemic range includes the waters that are east of the Rocky Mountains, several species have been introduced into the Pacific coast streams. However, the results have not been too good, because these voracious fishes prey upon young trout and salmon.

As food fishes, the catfishes present a controversial issue of considerable magnitude. As someone has said, and quite truthfully, I believe, "The catfishes are much like pickled olives — those who don't much like them, detest them."

The flesh of all of the catfishes is quite oily, and if they are taken from backwater slews, bayous, or other sluggish water where their food is "questionable," they are something less than savory. However, the flathead or goujon (one of the largest of the species) is an excellent food fish, as far as I am concerned, for it feeds primarily on "live food," i.e. other fish, crayfish, frogs, etc. and, as a result, its flesh is not rank but quite agreeable. I'm sure, however, that this opinion is not shared by everyone.

By and large, the most popular species among all of

the catfishes is the channel catfish, which is now being raised commercially on "catfish farms." With a controlled diet and stable water conditions, the fish becomes an excellent food fish.

See pages 80-81 on cleaning catfish.

Although the catfishes are cooked in several different ways, they are, to me at least, at their best when they are dipped in milk, rolled in corn meal, and fried quickly in deep, very hot fat.

Catfish should be served with Tartar Sauce (see sauce recipes), or pickles, turnip greens cooked with pig jowl, and, in the South "hush puppies" are a must. Corn bread or crackling bread pone are also staples.

"Hush Puppies"

The "hush puppy" is a traditional part of the fish fry in the South where this little corn pone originated. The story has it that when it was announced that there was to be a fish fry down in the woods, everybody showed up, and by "everybody" we mean the dogs too. Well, the gaiety of the occasion made the dogs bark and they got in the way of the busy cooks, so, to quiet the howling confusion, someone discovered that something to eat worked. And so, a barking dog was tossed a little corn pone with the admonition to "hush, puppy." And he did.

We might add that "hush puppies" and fried catfish go together like corn pone and pot liquor.

To prepare, sift twice 2 cups corn meal, 1 teaspoon salt, $\frac{1}{2}$ teaspoon black pepper and $1\frac{1}{2}$ teaspoons baking powder. Now add 1 large, finely chopped onion, 2 well beaten eggs, 4 tablespoons oil, and blend well with enough milk to make a stiff dough; shape into small pones about 3 inches long and less than 1 inch thick. (I have found that the best way to do this is to spoon about 3 tablespoons dough into the palm of the hand and squeeze it into the desired shape.)

Have the catfish frying in hot fat and drop the "hush puppies" into it and let them brown along with the fish.

The Eel

The eel is considered quite a delicacy in Europe, but we here in America have been slow to recognize this fact. No doubt its reptilian appearance has a great deal to do with our aversion to it, but the eel is not a reptile, it is a fish, and its flesh is more than palatable — it is delicious. There are many ways to prepare the eel but we would like to suggest only the two below.

Matelote of Eel

Skin, clean and cut into 2-inch lengths 1½ pounds eel. Put 3 tablespoons melted butter into a heavy stewpan and, when hot, drop in the pieces of eel; fry for 3 minutes, tossing and turning to insure even cooking. Now add ½ cup white wine, a pinch nutmeg, salt and pepper to taste, 1 or 2 sprigs parsley, the same of celery leaves, 1 small sliced onion, and pour over all 1 cup fish stock or hot water. Cut 6 mushrooms in thin slices and add to the eel; cook over a moderate fire for 30 minutes, or until the eel is very tender. Lift the fish from the broth and place on a hot platter. Cream 1 tablespoon flour with 1 tablespoon butter and add to broth; let all simmer for 3 minutes and pour over the eel.

Shrimp or crayfish tails that have been blanched in boiling water, shelled, and fried in a little butter, make an excellent garnish for this dish.

Eel in Deep Fat

Put 1 sliced onion, 1 sliced carrot, 3 sprigs parsley, a few celery leaves, a pinch freshly crushed black pepper, 1 bay leaf, 2 tablespoons vinegar, 1 scant tablespoon salt, and 4 cups cold water in a saucepan. Place over moderate

100

fire, let come to the boiling point, reduce heat and let simmer 5 minutes.

Prepare 2-inch pieces of eel and, when the herbs have simmered the 5 minutes, drop in the eel and cook 4 or 5 additional minutes. Remove from the fire and let the fish stand in the broth until it has cooled, then remove the eel, dip in beaten egg, roll in corn meal or craker dust, and fry in deep hot fat until it is a rich brown. Drain well on paper, and serve piping hot with Tartar Sauce (see sauce recipes), and garnish with wedges of lemon and sprigs of crisp parsley.

Carp, Sucker, Drum, and Buffalo

The carp is native to Asia and it was introduced into Europe centuries ago. It was brought to America from Europe in 1872. American anglers do not agree about the wisdom of adding the carp to the fishery resources of America, but it is too late to do anything about it, for today, it ramifies throughout the land, from creek to stream, from pond to lake.

In Europe, however, where superior fishes are less abundant than they are in this country, the carp is rather well thought of as a food fish, and it is possible, what with the ever increasing demands being put upon our fish-producing waters, that we, too, will learn to value the carp more as a food, and even as a sporting fish.

When taken from fairly decent water, and if properly prepared, carp is wholesome and nutritious. There are, however, embedded in the flesh more than the quota of small bones which cannot be avoided, even though fillets can be taken from the fish.

There are many species of suckers and they are well distributed in most of the fresh waters of the country. Like the carp, they are bony and, although they are important

101

food fishes in some localities, they are inferior to most of the table fishes.

The fresh-water drum, which is called sheepshead in the northern states, drum in the central portion of its range, and gaspergou in the South, is a good angler's fish, and not without some value as a food fish. Its flesh is coarse, rather tough, and, at times, a bit rank.

Another one of the coarse fishes that finds its way to the American table, either through the angler or the market fisherman, is the buffalo. It, too, is full of bones, but its flesh is superior to that of the carp.

Marinade for Coarse Fish

Because the flesh of the fishes mentioned above is ofttimes rank or "muddy" in flavor, it is well to marinate it before cooking. Prepare the marinade as follows:

For 3 or 4 pounds of fish, put through the food chopper two or three times, 1 large onion. Now add ½ cup vinegar, ½ cup cider, or water, ½ cup salt, 1 teaspoon black pepper, and a pinch of mace or nutmeg.

Remove the fillets from the fish, skin, and wash well, then arrange them in a flat, deep, enamelware, earthenware, or glass utensil. Pour the marinade over the fish and let stand for 4 hours, then remove the fillets and rinse thoroughly in cold water. No additional seasoning will be necessary because this was completed during the process of marinating, and so, the fish is now ready to be cooked in any way one chooses.

Although any of the coarser fishes mentioned above may be prepared the same as the recipes offered below for carp, the marinated fillets of all of them may also be cut into smaller portions, dipped in milk, rolled in corn meal, and fried in deep fat.

Baked Carp

Marinate 4 pounds fish fillets as suggested above. Chop or dice 1 green pepper, 3 sticks celery, 1 good-sized onion, 2 carrots, 1½ cups canned tomatoes; combine these vegetables and arrange in the bottom of a large baking dish or roasting pan. Roll the pieces of fish in flour, lay them on top of the vegetables, pour 4 tablespoons cooking oil over the fish, dust with paprika, and bake uncovered in a moderately hot oven (400°) for about 40 minutes, or until it is nicely browned. Baste occasionally with the liquid in the bottom of the pan.

To serve, arrange the fish in the center of a hot platter, surround with the vegetables, and send to the table piping hot.

Oven-Fried Carp Fillets

First marinate the required number of fillets as suggested above, dip them in beaten egg, and roll in fine bread crumbs. Place the pieces of fish on a well-greased baking tin and cook in a moderate oven for 30 to 40 minutes, according to the thickness of the fish.

To serve, place the fish in the center of a hot platter, surround with new potatoes that have first been boiled in their jackets, peeled, and browned lightly in a little butter. Garnish with wedges of lemon.

Turtles and Terrapins

It is too bad that many who think of turtles and terrapins as unfit for food have not tasted green turtle soup before passing judgment, for, unless prejudice paralyzes their taste buds, they will be compelled to admit they have experienced an epicurean delight.

The soft-shelled terrapin is a fresh-water species, and, although it is not as famous as the green turtle of the sea, it should not be overlooked by those who seek adventure

103

in good eating. Even the vicious looking snapping turtle is good food, and so are some of the tortoises which are the terrestrial species.

Terrapin Ragout

Clean one medium-sized or two small terrapins (preferably the soft-shelled species). (See pages 81-82 on cleaning terrapin.) Put the meat in a stewpan, cover with boiling water and simmer for 15 minutes.

In a frypan put 3 tablespoons melted butter, 1 diced onion and 1 clove finely minced garlic and cook 5 minutes, without browning, then blend in 1 rounded tablespoon flour, and add very slowly 1¼ cups of the broth in which the terrapins were cooked; stir until well blended. Add 1 bay leaf, a dash of nutmeg, 4 tablespoons sherry or 1 tablespoon vinegar, season with salt and a tiny dash of cayenne. Trim the meat from the bone and cut into small pieces; add to the broth and simmer gently for 30 minutes more. Serve piping hot.

Fried Young Terrapin

Clean and wipe thoroughly dry the required amount of terrapin meat. (See pages 81-82.) Dip the meat in milk, roll in cracker dust, and fry in deep hot fat. Drain well and serve while hot and crisp.

In case young terrapins are not available, the older specimens can be used, if they are first parboiled in salted water until they are tender. They should then be well drained, wiped dry, and prepared as young terrapins.

Frogs

Before cooking the large frogs (see page 83 on cleaning frogs), they should be cut into five pieces, that is, the hind legs, the forelegs, and the back. The hindquarters of the bullfrogs are apt to be a bit tough and stringy, and it is advisable to parboil them in tumbling salted water for 10 minutes, either before frying in deep fat, or broiling.

Broiled Frogs

Prepare the frogs as in the preceding recipe, lay them in a bowl, season with salt and pepper, and squeeze over them the juice of 1 lemon. Let the frogs marinate for 30 minutes; turn occasionally to expose all of the flesh to the marinade; remove from the marinade and wipe dry; brush over with oil and broil over a moderate fire for 4 or 5 minutes to the side.

To serve, arrange on a hot dish, dash with melted butter, sprinkle with finely chopped parsley, and send to the table.

The Marine Fishes

In the vast array of marine fishes there are hundreds of species which may well be considered among the finest food fishes in the world. However, if we attempted to list them in the order of their respective merit, we would become lost in a maze of confusion. We might start by saying, the several mackerels are excellent broiling fishes (see broiled whitefish, pages 86-87). Other superior food fishes include the sole, flounder, and halibut, to name three of the better known flat fishes. Fillets and steaks from these fish respond well to grilling, sautéing, baking, and frying in deep fat.

The following is an excellent recipe for preparing the fillets of any of the flat fishes.

Fillet of Sole With Blanched Oysters

Take the fillets from three sole (see pages 77-81 on cleaning fish), and wipe dry, then sauté lightly in hot butter. Place the fillets in a hot buttered baking dish, season with salt and pepper, and pour 4 tablespoons white

105

wine and 3 tablespoons mushroom liquid over them. Cover and cook 6 minutes in a fairly brisk oven; lift the fish out, drain them well, and arrange on a hot dish.

To the liquid left in the baking dish, add ½ cup chopped mushrooms, 12 blanched oysters, and 1 tablespoon melted butter. Cook over brisk fire 3 or 4 minutes. Garnish the fish with the oysters (see recipe for Oyster Garnish, page 113), pour over all the liquid and send to the table decorated with a few wedges of lemon.

The red snapper is an excellent representative of a family of food fishes which may be fried, sautéed, baked, or broiled; and because of their firm flaky flesh, they make delicious chowder, gumbo filé, or other Creole dishes. The recipe offered below is only one of many to which this superior fish lends itself.

Red Snapper a La Creole

Bone about 2 pounds of red snapper (see pages 77-81 on cleaning fish), and cut into small pieces that can be served easily.

Brown 1 medium-sized, finely chopped onion, add 1 tablespoon flour and blend until brown, mixing well. Now add 2 cups canned tomatoes, 2 sprigs chopped parsley, dash marjoram, 1 bay leaf, 1 small and finely minced clove garlic, dash allspice, salt and pepper to season, and mix thoroughly; then add juice of ½ lemon, dash cayenne, and ½ cup white wine. Simmer slowly for 12 minutes, adding hot water if the sauce gets too thick (it should be the consistency of thin cream). Put the pieces of fish into the sauce and continue to simmer until the fish is tender — this usually takes about 20 minutes.

Prepare ahead of time 12 small new potatoes by boiling them in their jackets; leave them whole, peel, and brown in a little butter.

To serve, place the fish in the center of a hot dish, pour

the sauce over them, and garnish with the browned new potatoes.

The beautiful, brilliantly polished, silver-and-gold pompanos inhabit the warmer seas. They are not too abundant, and to the angler they fail to come up to the requirements of a sporting fish because they rarely take the hook. Because of the contour of their bodies, the pompanos have been given their Spanish name which means grape leaf.

As a table delicacy, the pompanos have few equals; and they should always be broiled.

Broiled Pompano

See recipe for broiled whitefish, pages 86-87.

Serve with this dish, buttered asparagus, creamed new potatoes, and wedges of lemon.

Part XII

Sauces and Garnishes

Bechamel Sauce

Into a deep saucepan or frypan put 3 tablespoons melted butter. Place over slow fire and add 1 finely minced carrot, 1 finely minced onion, and ½ cup finely diced cured ham. Simmer gently for 20 minutes, without browning. Now lift the vegetables and ham out with a spatula and put them in a bowl and set aside.

In the same saucepan put 3 more tablespoons melted butter and 2 tablespoons flour; cream into a smooth paste; add gradually 1½ cups milk, stirring continually. Now put the vegetables and the ham in the saucepan, add 1 small bay leaf, a dash each of nutmeg and thyme, 6 whole peppercorns, a sprig of parsley, a few celery leaves and half a clove of finely minced garlic. Season with salt and simmer for 45 minutes, stirring frequently to prevent sticking. Strain through a fine sieve, set aside to cool, and use as required.

This sauce is excellent when added to braised squirrel, grouse, or doves.

Egg Sauce

Put 2 tablespoons butter in a frypan; add 2 tablespoons flour and blend to a smooth paste, without browning. Now stir in 1 cup milk, 2 teaspoons finely minced onion, a dash of cloves and a pinch of black pepper; blend with wire whisk or a wooden spoon over a very low fire until perfectly smooth and the right consistency. When the sauce has cooked long enough, grate or finely chop 2 hard-cooked eggs into it.

Serve this sauce with baked, broiled, or sautéed fish.

Horseradish Sauce

Cream 2 level tablespoons butter with 2 tablespoons of good hot horseradish; add 1 tablespoon very thick cream and ½ teaspoon lemon juice; blend together and put in a cool place until needed.

This sauce goes well with any broiled or roasted game.

Londonderry Sauce

First cut the rind of ½ lemon into julienne shaped pieces and blanch for 3 minutes in boiling water. Now put about 3 ounces good port wine in a saucepan; add ½ teaspoon freshly crushed black pepper and the blanched lemon rind; let boil for not more than 3 minutes, then add ½ cup currant or any other tart jelly, and simmer until well blended.

Serve in a separate dish with broiled or roasted wild fowl or venison.

Mexican Sauce

Vein and seed 3 chimayo peppers and 3 small hot

chilies. Put them in a saucepan and add 2 cloves garlic that have been bruised into a paste with the point of a knife, and ½ teaspoon cumin seeds; cover with boiling water and let simmer 10 minutes over a slow fire. Remove from the fire and scrape the pulp from the pepper and chili skins, discard the skins and set the rest aside.

Into another saucepan put 2 tablespoons melted butter, when hot, add 1 tablespoon sesame seeds and 3 tablespoons pine (piñon) nuts that have either been run through a food chopper or pounded. Toast the nuts in the butter for 2 minutes, then add juice of 1 small orange and 1 lime, 1 cup canned tomatoes, the peppers and chilies with the liquid in which they were cooked, 1 heaping tablespoon raisins, 3 cloves, 3 thin slices orange peel, ¼ teaspoon cinnamon, and a dash of ginger; season lightly with salt. If necessary, thin with hot stock or water. Simmer gently for 45 minutes or 1 hour; just before removing from the fire, add 1 tablespoon grated sweet chocolate and blend it in well.

The sauce is now ready to serve with broiled or roasted turkey, grouse, pheasant, quail, rabbit, etc.

Mint Sauce

Take 1 cup finely chopped fresh mint leaves and add ½ cup water and ½ cup stock, 4 tablespoons vinegar, 1 teaspoon salt and 1 heaping tablespoon powdered sugar. Stir well and let stand for at least 1 hour before serving.

When ready to serve, pour into a sauce dish and serve with roasted or broiled venison, goose, or duck.

Tartar Sauce

Put 1 cup mayonnaise in a mixing bowl; add 2 tablespoons finely minced or grated onions, 1 tablespoon lemon juice and, if you like, 1 tablespoon capers. Blend well.

Serve this sauce with broiled, sautéed, baked or fried fish.

111

Apple Garnish

Select 6 firm, tart apples (preferably winesaps), leave the peeling on, square the blossom end and core, then cut in ½-inch thick slices crosswise, and sauté in butter. Turn with a cake turner, being careful not to break the apple; sprinkle each slice with brown sugar and dust with cinnamon, allspice, and cloves.

Use as a garnish for roasted duck, goose, or venison.

Banana Garnish

Select the required number of firm, not overly ripe bananas (one to a serving). Peel carefully and cut in two, lengthwise. For each banana put 1 tablespoon melted butter in a flat baking pan and when hot lay in the bananas, cut side down, then turn, sprinkle brown sugar on the flat side and dust with cinnamon, allspice and cloves. Put to bake in moderate oven until slightly clear and tender.

Use as a garnish for fried, broiled, or roasted quail, pheasant, grouse, turkey, or partridge.

Liver and Mushroom Garnish

Carefully remove the gall bladders from 6 or 8 grouse, pheasant, duck, squirrel, rabbit, or other game livers; season the livers with salt and pepper, roll them in a little oil, then grill in a hot frypan for 1 minute to each side. Add 6 finely chopped mushrooms and cook 2 minutes longer, then add 1½ cups stock and ½ cup Madeira wine. Simmer 8 minutes and use to garnish any broiled or roasted game.

Okra Garnish

Select the required number of tender okra pods, cut off the stem end and sauté in hot butter over a slow fire until tender. Turn the pods often to expose them to an even heat, and be sure the butter does not burn.

112

Serve as a garnish with broiled or roasted game.

Oyster Garnish

Take 6 or 8 good-sized fresh oysters, flatten slightly, dip in milk, roll in cracker dust, season with salt and pepper, and put to broil on a well-greased grill for 3 minutes to each side.

Arrange each oyster on canapés of thin buttered toast, sprinkle with chopped parsley, and serve with roasted duck, grouse, goose, etc.

Tomato-Shrimp Garnish

Chop 1 green pepper very fine and put in a saucepan with 1 chopped fresh tomato, or ½ cup canned tomatoes; add 2 tablespoons melted butter and 18 cooked and finely chopped shrimp. (If shrimp are not available and crayfish are, use the crayfish tails.) Season with salt and pepper and cook 10 minutes.

Serve with any broiled or sautéed fish.

Maitre d'Hotel Butter

Cream 2 level tablespoons butter and add gradually ½ teaspoon salt and a dash freshly crushed white pepper. Blend with this 1 tablespoon lemon juice and 1 tablespoon finely chopped parsley. Keep in a cool place.

Serve with broiled quail, grouse, pheasant, snipe, duck, venison chops, broiled trout, whitefish, etc.

Part XIII

Appendices

Appendix A

Making Camp

In this modern world we live in, the ability to get along outdoors is almost a lost art. Yesterday, America was a frontier nation and self-reliance and resourcefulness came as standard equipment; but we tamed this land in a hurry and the majority of our rugged sportsmen of today "rough" it in luxury. And they find it easy to do so because the recreational trails across the nation are lined with dude ranches, cabins, and public campgrounds where the essentials for a reasonable amount of comfort are at hand. Added to this is the easy access to any area via airplane, helicopter, jeep or snowmobile.

But there are individuals who still want to go out and beyond these established conveniences and, for these hardy souls who prefer to enjoy more rugged recreation outdoors,

115

a knowledge of woodcraft and good camping is important. For instance, when selecting a campsite, especially one that is to be used for a few days or weeks, it is most important to consider several factors which will contribute to both safety and comfort. Perhaps first and most important is the location of a supply of fresh, uncontaminated drinking water for, even in remote areas, this can present a problem and, if near human habitation, extreme caution should be taken. Where there is the slightest doubt, all drinking water should be boiled; if this isn't convenient, chlorine tablets should be added. Even when camping near a clear, moving trout stream in a remote area, a check of the stream far above camp should be made, for there could be the carcass of a beaver, sheep, deer, cow or other animal in or near the stream.

If camp is to be made on a stream it should be on high ground and well above the highest floodmark. Too, low ground or a slough should not be between camp and the upland; otherwise, there is danger of being marooned during high water. And the ground where camp is to be pitched should be studied for signs of flooding along the stream where drifts of debris have been left. When possible, local information should be obtained about the stream and its flood stages.

Before a spot for the tent, fire, and camp table is selected, all overhead timber should be examined. Pitching camp under dead trees, trees that are partially dead, or those with hollow trunks and dead limbs that might fall or split off during a windstorm, should be avoided; a windfall can damage equipment, and it might take a life.

In setting up a summer camp, the tent door should face in the direction of the prevailing breeze and be free from crowding timber and brush so as to catch the sweep of the wind. The morning sun isn't uncomfortably warm, and the tent should be pitched so that it will be in the shade from midmorning until evening; a tent gets mighty warm

116

when the afternoon sun beats down on it for even a short time.

If bedrolls are to be put on the ground or tent floor, all rocks and sticks should be cleared away and the ground leveled. The tent should be well anchored with stakes and guy ropes, the walls and top should be tight, and nothing should touch the tent on the inside because water will come through when it rains. Ditching around the tent is a good idea, too, for water is carried off in this way and it helps to prevent water from running under the tent floor or into the tent during a heavy rain.

It is also impotant to locate a good supply of wood. Hardwood is much the best for it burns longer and creates hotter coals. Standing dead timber is preferable because wood that has been lying on the ground is usually punky and worthless, except for the night fire. A supply of light tinder such as dry bark, broomweed, and evergreen boughs, along with extra wood, should be stored in a sheltered spot where it will keep dry.

An ax, which must be included in the camp equipment, can be one of the most dangerous tools for, if one gets careless even for a moment, a split foot or an injured shin might mean real trouble, especially if camp is in a remote area. Even the first-aid kit could do little good in such a case.

The campfire should not be built upwind from the tent, otherwise sparks might ignite both tent and bedding. And building a trench fireplace or rimming the firebed with rocks will contain the fire. Many rocks (especially those that are gathered near the stream) will burst when hot, and they are apt to send slivers flying with enough force to cause injury. Guarding against this is only a sensible precaution. Too, leaving a fire burning when away from camp for any length of time is unwise for it might get loose and start a brush, grass, or forest fire. The national forest authorities are very strict about this, and it is wise to follow

117

their instructions to the letter, especially those relating to fires and clean camps.

Autumn and winter camps present an entirely different problem and protection on the south side of heavy timber, windfalls, a hillock, or a sheltering bank can add to camping pleasure. Of course, the locality and weather have a great deal to do with the selection of a comfortable campsite, and good judgment can avoid problems that might otherwise occur.

In short, the camper who wants to be comfortable locates safe drinking water, observes weather conditions, establishes safeguards against rain, floods, rough winter weather, fires, falling timber, and too much heat or cold. With proper equipment, common sense, and good food, camping cannot only be a great experience, it can also be high and unforgettable adventure.

Appendix B

Fires

Our world today is a world of science and technology. Man has walked on the moon; he knows the depths of the sea; he knows the age of rocks. But he still looks into a campfire with wonder in his eyes, and, if there is wonder, there is more to come.

The fire is usually the prelude to a nightmare of difficulties which torment the inexperienced outdoor cook. In fact, it has been said that a camper can be judged by his fire. And, there is no doubt but that much of the success of outdoor cookery depends upon the correct management of the fire.

Experienced campers use quite a variety of fires, and a knowledge of them is most valuable to any camper, for it helps to contribute to his comfort. Building and managing

118

the right sort of fire at the right time, and using the best fuel that is available, are the keys to a good campfire.

The wise camper keeps a supply of dry kindling stowed away, but, even so, there are times when he has no dry tinder, and he has to build a fire in the rain. If there is pitch pine or red cedar around, the job is greatly simplified for, with an ax, or heavy hunting knife, "fat" pine can be split or shaved from an old stump; and, if one finds red cedar, one can chop into its center and shave or split off a handful of slivers. If there is neither pine nor red cedar, the driest fuel that can be found should be used. Very old softwood trees, especially where they lean, often have dry, loose bark on the underside which can be used to advantage.

Of course, weather and locality have much to do with the success of building a fire in the rain. If there is only a shower to contend with, there is little difficulty in locating dry wood; but a prolonged wet spell makes things more difficult.

Wood that is lying flat on the ground should not be gathered for it is apt to be too wet to burn. Sheltered spots should be found and every tiny sprig that seems dry enough to ignite should be saved. Softwood that usually grows along the streams, and most driftwood that is found along the banks make poor fuel, for, even though this wood ignites quickly, it soon burns down to a pile of worthless ashes. It is also well to keep in mind that box elder, poplar, tamarack, cedar, hemlock, and the soft pines pop and crackle a great deal when they burn; for this reason, they should be watched so that flying sparks which might ignite leaves, grass, tent, or bedrolls can be checked.

In selecting a place to build a fire, look for a sheltered bank, a rock cliff or ledge, a leaning tree or the protecting arms of a spreading spruce. Be careful to arrange all of the light tinder on a supporting stick and slant down wind. This allows the blaze to be carried up the matchstick in the cupped hands. Hold the blaze on the upwind side of the pile of tinder and keep it protected with the cupped hands.

119

If the blaze wavers and begins to fail, feed it with the smallest and driest tinder available. Keep the blaze protected until it takes hold, then add larger sticks, being careful not to smother the flame with sticks that are too heavy.

There are several things about fires that should never be forgotten: (1) Watch them closely at all times; (2) bank them carefully at night; and (3) put them out when breaking camp. Not a single spark should ever be overlooked.

Every experienced camper has his favorite fires, and the following are mine.

The Log Fire

The log fire is both simple and practical. Lay two 4-foot green logs parallel on the ground and around 10 or 12 inches apart, or close enough so they will accommodate the kettles and the skillets. The logs should be about 8 inches in diameter. Place them crosswise the prevailing wind and put small rocks under the ends of the windward log to allow the fire to draw better. Actually, these rocks can be used as dampers by raising the logs to increase the heat and lowering them to reduce it.

The log fire is excellent when using the Dutch oven for baking or braising, because it provides ample coals. Too, coals can be lifted from the firebed and set to one side where the oven can be placed over them. Thus, the bread can bake on the side while the balance of the meal is being prepared over the main fire.

The Lug Pole Fire

A good lug pole, or fire crane arrangement for the cooking fire can be built as follows: Drive stout, green, forked stakes about 5 feet apart and directly opposite one another, on either side of where the fire is to be built. The crotches should be 30 inches above the ground. Cut a green lug pole

120

stick 2 inches thick and long enough to span the fire by reaching from one crotch to the other, and with some to spare.

Since the lug pole is free at both ends, simply lift one end and slip it through the bail of the cooking kettle; return the lug pole to the crotch and adjust the kettle to the desired position over the firebed. The right heat is governed by the management of the fire under the kettle.

This same lug pole arrangement can be used when roasting a duck, a goose, or a venison roast. Attach a wire to the bird or the roast, and suspend from the lug pole above the bed of coals, and manage the fire to assure even heat while cooking.

The Trench Fire

When the wind plays havoc with a fire, which is often, a trench fire is best. To build such a fire, dig a trench that runs with the wind; make it deepest at the windward end and slant it upward toward the leeward end. Build most of the fire in the deeper end, for the wind will carry the heat leeward. In case there is too much draft, pile some of the dirt that was moved when the trench was dug in a semicircle around the windward end, or place rocks or logs in the same position.

The wind is usually much stronger in flat country where only small brush is available for fuel, and it is under these conditions that the trench fire is very satisfactory, for it enables one to get the most heat out of the light fuel.

Where the country is rough and broken, it is unnecessary to dig a trench for it is a rather simple matter to find a cut bank creek, a dry wash, a rock ledge, or other protected spots where a fire can be built and the wind will offer no problem.

The Campfire

In an established camp, especially if the weather is rough,

it is wise to make the campfire independent from the cooking fire. This is because the campfire is usually too big and decidedly too hot to accommodate the variety of cookery that is necessary to insure the greatest pleasure of camp life — good food. There are times, however, when a few shovelsful of bright coals from the campfire are needed to augment the cooking fire, so it is wise to tend this extra fire at all times.

A few sizeable green logs should always be kept handy for backlogs. Some of the best green woods to use are box elder, aspen, poplar, water oak, sourwood, and sycamore. None of these woods will burn when they are green, especially during the spring and summer months when the sap is up.

When camping for several days, the overnight fire can be held by banking the coals with ashes. Then the breakfast fire can be kindled easily by simply opening the bank of ashes which exposes the live coals, then laying a handful of dry tinder on them, and following with heavier sticks later.

When the time comes to break camp and to kill the fire, remember — no campfire should ever die without talk of tomorrow.

Appendix C

Utensils

It is not only impossible but impractical for the camper to carry many conveniences with him. However, whatever he plans to take should be carefully thought out, for a hodgepodge of utensils that are gathered together willy-nilly are apt to be most disappointing.

A study of the catalogues of the reputable outfitters will indicate a good variety of practical camping equipment. It might be well to point out, however, that aluminum,

122

although light, isn't too serviceable, for it dents easily, food sticks to it readily when exposed to dry heat, and coffee cups stay blistering hot, even after the brew has cooled. And the aluminum frypan is an abomination, for everything cooked in it sticks, and it soon warps.

Steelware is not only serviceable but it is very strong, if it has been stamped out of solid pieces of steel and doubly tinned. The frypans and kettles made from this material are most satisfactory.

For the most part, tinware is light, very cheap, and extremely flimsy. Utensils made from this material aren't too satisfactory for they soon rust, and the soldered joints give considerable grief because they fail to withstand campfire heat.

Enamelware is very desirable in many respects. True, it will chip, especially in cold weather and if it is subjected to much abuse, but even so, with the exception of the frypan, it is most practical.

When it comes to camp equipment, every seasoned camper has his likes and dislikes. For example, when it is at all feasible and possible, I am never without my Dutch oven. Even though the reflector baker, especially the folding type, is lighter, more compact, and more portable, I still prefer the Dutch oven.

The Dutch oven is an all purpose utensil, for its heavy cast-iron metal permits an even heat that is unsurpassed in any other utensil. It is because of this that it can be used as a frypan, especially when frying in deep fat; it can be used to bake breads, or fruit cobblers; it can be used to prepare meat, fowl, and fish.

On the other hand, the reflector type oven is light and easily packed, but because it is made of thin metal, the heat gets to the food more directly, which isn't desirable when baking meats, etc. As for the baking of breads, especially baking powder breads, the more direct action of the heat is desirable, and it is here that the reflector is at its

123

best. True, the heat can be controlled, but for delicious foods, the Dutch oven is greatly superior.

Stewpots should be low, wide-mouthed pails with tight fitting lids. Their sizes should be say of 2-, 4-, and 6-quart capacities, and they should nest in one another. The wide pail permits quicker boiling because the heat comes in contact with a wider heating surface. These pails also make good mixing bowls, and they can be used to carry water in.

As to the frypan, it is better to take along one large pan than two or three small ones; and one made from strong pressed steel will prove to be most satisfactory.

The cups, plates, and a few small nesting sauce dishes should be of stainless steel, as should the knives, forks and spoons. Unless hunting knives are carried by members of the party, a good, heavy, all-purpose knife should be included in the equipment.

The salt and pepper shakers should be of aluminum.

There is no utensil more important to the camper than the coffee pot. If boiled coffee is to be made, avoid a thin aluminum pot, or one that is seamed, because the action of direct heat on thin aluminum is disastrous to good coffee, and a seamed pot soon collects the rancid oils which, when mixed with the brew itself, cause a most unpalatable flavor. If it is made of fairly heavy aluminum, the drip type coffee maker is an excellent utensil and, by and large, it will make better coffee than the boiling pot — at least, it is more foolproof. Too, if it is thoroughly scalded and sunned, it can be used for brewing tea.

If there is room for only one wire grill, it is best to take the standing type with legs that fold up when packed. Be sure to select one that has the electro-welded construction, and one of a size that is large enough to accommodate the coffee pot, frypan, and a kettle at the same time, or about 14 x 20 inches.

The double grill, with the long handles, is very useful

124

for broiling and toasting, but the standing grill can be used not only for this type cooking, but for so much else besides.

The can opener, several small cans with tight fitting lids (to be used for seasonings other than salt and pepper), and a supply of pot rags and dish towels should not be left out. As for a rolling pin, a good substitute can be made by simply peeling a green elm, aspen, or any sweetwood stick about 14 inches long and two inches thick.

It is fun and challenging to be resourceful when in camp. If you have never tried it, I hope you will, soon.

Appendix D

Provisions

It would be useless and impractical to set down an itemized list of provisions as a guide for the campers of today for, with transportation like it is, something to eat is available at almost any crossroads.

For those who want to pack in to remote areas, however, it might be well to make a few suggestions. Remember that water is heavy, which makes canned foods too heavy and bulky to take on such trips; but on boat or canoe trips, these foods may be included, provided there are no long or difficult portages.

Many of the dehydrated foods that are on the market today are usable, and some are better than others. There are dried fruits, corn, milk, and beans (keep in mind that it is next to impossible to cook dried beans at an altitude above 4,000 feet); and, less satisfactory but obtainable, are desiccated eggs, green vegetables, and potatoes. Avoid taking foods that contain the same nutritional and vitamin values, such as, say, both potatoes and breads, or dried prunes and apricots, etc.

It is also well to remember that unless the camp is at high altitude, cured meats will not hold too long.

Lard is an excellent shortening for baking, but vegetable compounds will not get rancid as quickly nor will they melt as rapidly when the weather is warm.

A most delightful syrup can be made from any of the wild cherries that might be found in the area where you are camped. Place the fruit in a saucepan, cover with water and cook slowly until it begins to pop open, then pour all into a clean cloth sack, tie a cord around the top of the sack and let the juice drain down into a utensil.

To make the syrup, put equal parts cherry juice and sugar in a saucepan, let come to the boil slowly, and continue to cook until the syrup thickens. The syrup will hold if it is kept in a reasonably cool place; and a fruit jar, or a quart bottle with cork or screw cap, serve as adequate containers.

If other wild fruits are in season, preserves and jams can be made easily simply by adding sugar to the raw fruit and cooking slowly until it begins to thicken, which usually takes from 15 to 30 minutes.

Coffee and tea are the beverages most thoroughly enjoyed by all campers and both are carried easily, even though tea is lighter. It might be borne in mind that coffee is very volatile and that the oil in the coffee berry will become rancid in a short while. To preserve the deliciousness of coffee, it should be kept in a friction-top can or fruit jar.

Cocoa is also a delightful drink and, although it fails to give the "lift" that either coffee or tea does, it is much more nourishing.

Appendix E

Taking Care of Yourself When Lost

To some it might seem rather absurd to think of anyone getting lost in a country so civilized and populated as

America, but it is a very simple matter, especially for the city dweller. In truth, I have known individuals who could get lost in their own backyard, so to speak. And so, perhaps, at the outset, we could do no better than to offer a few bits of advice to all those who might find themselves lost in a wilderness some day.

Above all, keep cool. Don't lose your head or become frightened, for it will only add to your confusion and waste needed energy.

If you have companions, stay with them, for you can help one another to hold on to your courage.

Conserve your energy and food, and utilize all edible wild foods at hand. Seek shelter at night; sleep as well as possible; avoid unwarranted risks and exposure.

You may pride yourself on having an instinctive sense of direction. Beware, for this can lead you astray. There is no such sense; we have been civilized too long. Through experience and accurate observation a highly developed sense of direction may be acquired, even to the point of becoming almost subconscious, but it is never infallible.

When possible, always carry with you into the wilderness a reliable compass. Make certain that you know which end of the needle points toward the north; if the instrument isn't marked it should be. On clear days there will be no need for a compass but when it is cloudy you want to be sure that you aren't walking south when you want to be going north. If you don't have a compass and there is no sun, moon or stars, it is possible to make a few observations which, if correctly interpreted, will set you square with the world about you. For example: If you are in a fairly open country and the day is cloudy, the point of a knife blade or a sharpened twig held vertically against the thumbnail will cast a shadow. The shadow, of course, will fall in the opposite direction from the sun. The tops of trees that stand above the forest, especially conifers such as pine, spruce, etc., will be leaning away from the prevailing wind, which is often from the north. And look for lichen which will be on the north side of the tree trunks. Where there are sand dunes or snowdrifts, remember that their steep sides are the windward sides.

Never cross a fence, if you haven't done so in your wandering.

When going into an area (that is, of course, before you have become lost) observe carefully the direction in which the streams are flowing; and if there are hills, ridges, valleys and mountains, note their positions in relation to the points of the compass. Remember, in a trackless wilderness, streams are highways for the man who is lost, and if you follow them, you are fairly certain to find habitation.

If you know that a searching party will be out looking for you, establish yourself in one place and signal your location, using a fire at night, smoke or a piece of cloth (preferably white) as a banner during the day, and, if you can spare the ammunition, fire a shot occasionally.

If you are in arid country, try to find a water hole, for someone will very likely find you, because both cattle and game trails lead to water. Follow the main stem of the trail — that is, where one or more trails converge, follow the main stem. To find such trails go along the rim of the tablelands where they break off into a swale, valley or canyon, and you will very likely come upon a "live" trail that leads to water. Strips or patches of green vegetation often indicate water holes, but in the desert region beware of drinking from springs where there is an absence of green vegetation, for such springs are usually contaminated with harmful or poisonous salts and are, therefore, dangerous.

Avoid sunstroke, extreme cold and snow blindness. Overexertion will cause heatstroke; guard against this; keep the head covered. In sub-zero temperatures, guard against frostbite; watch the ears, nose, face, fingers and toes. Very gentle manipulation of the affected parts, or immersing in water that is slightly above the freezing point, will usually restore the frostbitten members to normal. If you or your companions become drowsy, keep moving and try to find

128

a cut bank, windfall or any available shelter where a fire can be built. Conserve your matches and keep them dry. If you doze, a kick on the shin or a vigorous slap or two might make you mad, but it might also save your life.

Epilogue

The way of life of all wild creatures of both field and stream presents a study that is inexhaustible and always fascinating. Hunting and fishing are productive of a great deal of genuine adventure and it is lamentable that many sportsmen allow their enthusiasm to wane with the bagging of the quarry for, in so doing, they overlook an opportunity to experience the finer aspects of hunting and fishing.

And so, before you lay this book aside, stop for just a moment to ponder these thoughts: When you kill a wild creature just to see if you can, do you feel any respect for yourself, or do you merely admire your prowess? Do you regard it as incongruous to maintain an honorable respect for yourself and at the same time have a genuine respect for the creatures you hunt and fish for? To me, the two are more than compatible — they are essentially the same, for you cannot have one without the other; and, if we believe in the nobility of man, then we should demonstrate it afield and elsewhere.

During the years I have gone afield I have held steadfast to the philosophy that when I cease to respect the trout that takes my fly — the big buck who eludes me in the rough canyon — the quail that freezes tight for my pointer, I'll stop bothering them.

Last November, during the quail season, I finished a day's hunt on a rimrock in the Kansas Flint Hills overlooking a small valley. The sun was dropping into a sea of brown and gray and mauve. Below me I saw the stream, the fields where the corn had come to ear again, the valley wrapped in the blue haze of autumn, and twilight slipping long, shadowy fingers through the tall, motionless trees. Sparrows twittered in the nearby bush and crows flecked the distant horizon. From far off the lowing of cattle and the smell of good earth came up to greet me. Then I remembered that it was the season of Thanksgiving, and all about me, above me and below me, was America, that I was free and that free men like me had fought to keep the freedom that lay like a benediction over, under, around, and within me at that moment.

This is my answer to the question: Of what value is our recreation afield?